AF328719

Changemaker

~~CHANGE~~

JACQUELINE
CORBELLI

Changemaker
~~CHANGE~~

A *Modern* ^ PLAYBOOK FOR

CREATING *Personal* ~~REAL~~ IMPACT

and

Transformational Change

WILEY

*In loving memory of my nana and with deep affection
and appreciation for my mom.*

Contents

I have been impressed with the urgency of doing.
Knowing is not enough; we must apply.
Being willing is not enough; we must do.

—Leonardo da Vinci

Foreword

In 1963, at the height of the Cold War, President John F. Kennedy was determined to move the world toward peace. In his famous Peace Speech on June 10, 1963, he defined an approach to problem-solving: "By defining our goal more clearly, by making it seem more manageable and less remote, we help all people to see it, to draw hope from it, and to move irresistibly toward it."

In this wonderful guide for today's entrepreneurs and changemakers, Jacqueline Corbelli offers a cutting-edge handbook for defining our goals more clearly, making them more manageable and less remote, and thereby driving scaled and effective solutions. Her own business leadership at the intersection of media and technology, her leadership in fighting extreme poverty, and her creation of a powerful global platform for sustainable development are inspiring case studies and powerful guides to achieving bold goals.

This book describes a systematic methodology for changemaking, whether in business, civil society, or the public sphere. Corbelli guides us through a step-by-step process.

First, as JFK recommended, define one's goals more clearly. This is crucial: think ahead, imagine the desired future, and prepare to build a roadmap to that future. Second, chart out a pathway to the desired future and the likely obstacles that will be encountered along that pathway. Third, create an implementation plan, with a special focus on the powerful technologies that can be harnessed to reach the goal. Fourth, network with others, since solutions to complex challenges require the integration of diverse areas of knowledge, production, and innovation. Corbelli's highly innovative SustainChain offers an AI-empowered, online platform for businesses and academia to create the ecosystems they need for success. Fifth, be ready to pivot. New technologies emerge, markets shift, and unforeseen obstacles arise. Don't despair but do pivot. As Corbelli's own experiences show, plans are crucial but must continually be updated to achieve success.

Her guidance recalls the wisdom of Dwight D. Eisenhower, who led the Allies to victory in World War II. He famously said, "Plans are useless, but planning is indispensable." Plan—but be ready to adapt and pivot along the way. Corbelli makes this point powerfully.

I have been the lucky beneficiary of Jacquie Corbelli's enormous talents, insight, drive, and commitment to a better world. I have learned from her entrepreneurial flair as a business leader in new media, as chair of the board of Millennium Promise Alliance during the implementation of the Millennium Villages Project, and as the innovator of the SustainChain platform to support the sustainable development goals.

Corbelli is a builder of the future we want and need on our crowded planet, and a wonderful guide and coach for today's changemakers.

Jeffrey D. Sachs

Economics professor, author, and global

leader in sustainable development

Introduction

Have you ever dreamed of having the personal ability to help reshape the world? To break down the walls that keep us from fixing big problems like tackling global poverty, reducing wealth gaps, advancing social equity, addressing climate change, and halting global conflict?

Without a doubt, putting our passions, desires, and intentions into action is an incredibly fraught road of twists, turns, and steep climbs, where the best tools and navigation can still fail, even when they mean the difference between failure and success. It's not surprising that our ability to make a difference and having enough self-belief and confidence to attempt it are often a sea apart. What makes it worse is that the complex nature we observe in others' failures stops most of us in our tracks before we even get off the blocks.

At the same time, whether it is global change, business transformation, or community or personal well-being, the biggest landmarks on the journey to consequential action are surprisingly similar, and your awareness of them, proactive planning for them, and commitment to flexibly managing them can give you the burst of confident energy you need to get started.

In this book, I share an overall framework that will make seemingly impossible challenges possible—both within and outside the realms of business, in world matters like poverty, sustainability, and in everyday life. It begins and ends with a very specific thought process and set of steps that have proven over and over to achieve real, lasting impact and change. All are rooted in the basic premise that the answers we seek, whether personally or as part of a bigger picture, are often hiding in plain sight; that even the most intimidating challenges can frequently be easily broken down into smaller pieces and a series of actionable next steps; and that when this approach is combined with responsible uses of today's most advanced technologies, we can achieve transformational change, for ourselves and for others.

This book is based on my firsthand experiences and accomplishments with the purpose of emboldening all with a desire to wrestle with problems that appear too big to conquer, in life and in the world. It puts forth a ready-set-go playbook for tackling the paralysis that steals our hope and confidence to face major challenges by providing proven strategies and a roadmap that can guide you toward forging your own personal impact.

It's my hope that the themes reflected in these pages will allow you to easily embrace this framework and replicate it, step by step, in your own lives, and for it to serve as an easy reference as you go. If I can inspire you to have the confidence not just to make changemaking a hobby, but perhaps to also consider yourself capable of having an impact on a world scale, I will consider this book a great success.

And with that, let's get started.

Changemaker

<del>CHANGE</del>

Fundamentals

The following chapters provide you with a framework for tapping into your inner changemaker and introduce the key ingredients for creating your own personal playbook for solving challenges in your life and in the world. Once the journey is complete, three major ingredients will come together to put the needed capabilities into place:

- The mental model to tap into your own inherent potential to be a changemaker
- The process discipline to maintain necessary focus and prioritization for your actions
- The significance and versatility of utilizing the most modern technologies as tools to elevate and supercharge our own natural human capabilities

The book begins the journey by exploring the paths by which we can teach ourselves to see with different eyes and free ourselves from the notion that complexity will prevent us from reaching our goals. We'll also observe the levels of creativity generated by the simple act of breaking down challenges into more digestible pieces.

Part I lays the groundwork for the changemaker's playbook through two chapters:

- Chapter 1 provides the foundation by showing how to discover the extraordinary in the ordinary, illustrates the hope that springs up when you take the first bold step forward, and lays down the myth of impossibility.
- Chapter 2 shows the promise of using a structured yet flexible set of steps to help frame the way you think about and approach change, and how it can arm you to face challenges with clarity and a strategic mindset.

1 | The Path to Creating New Futures

The journey begins with this powerful idea: Solutions to even the most difficult challenges often *hide in plain sight.* This may seem hard to believe. However, I will give you many reasons to see the truth of this statement in the following pages. Through the examples and illustrations I share you will not only understand why this is so, but you'll also have a solid foundation for understanding how it applies to solving real-world problems, on a personal level and a global one as well. You may even find yourself with a new desire to play a part. For now, I'll begin to build that foundation very simply. Think about the last time you lost your keys or your phone. You searched everywhere, only to find it right on the countertop—or, if you're like me, sometimes right in your own hand. These everyday moments aren't just a function of forgetfulness; they also highlight an important truth: What we see—or don't see—often depends on where we focus our attention.

hiding in plain sight, idiom: Refers to objects or solutions that are easily overlooked due to the simple and uncomplicated nature of their location.

As simplistic as it may seem, this same idea also applies to contributing to major change as well. As you are about to see from the following examples, sometimes solutions to problems are around us, but we miss them because we're not looking for them in the right way. Throughout history, major shifts often began with someone suddenly recognizing something that was there all along. The key both then, and which applies to this day, is in learning *how to see* it—notice the opportunities that others overlook, question the assumptions that keep problems locked in place, and most importantly act when the moment presents itself.

The pages ahead will help you explore how you can develop this kind of awareness and think differently about the true extent of your own capabilities. There are a wide variety illustrations within to show you how I did so, and a DIY way to achieve it yourself. You'll also find a workbook at the end to hone your skills. So let's get started by first considering some real-world examples of how seeing differently leads to lasting and even historic change.

Learning to See

One of the greatest and most groundbreaking examples of seeing the same thing differently in human history is Sir Isaac Newton's discovery of gravity. For centuries, people experienced gravity firsthand—when you trip over a tree root, for instance, you fall straight to the ground. But it took Newton's relentless curiosity and determination to transform part of our everyday experience into a scientific law that captured the very essence of gravity. Newton's work proved that the missing piece to understanding this natural force observed for thousands of years had been hiding in plain sight all along. In his ability to carefully observe, question, and connect the dots between seemingly separate phenomena he uncovered one of the most fundamental principles of our universe.

Newton's discovery was much more than just an explanation of why things fall—it also revealed gravity as a universal force that not only governs the drop of an apple from a tree but the motion of planets around the sun (National Geographic, 2022). This particular revelation laid the groundwork for countless other scientific breakthroughs that we rely on today, making possible everything from precise flight path calculations that enable us to travel across the globe in mere hours, to the development of space travel, where understanding gravitational pull is crucial to launching rockets and exploring beyond our atmosphere.

The implications didn't stop there. Newton's work also allowed us to solve practical challenges, like reliable access to electricity through innovations such as hydroelectric power, which harnesses gravity-driven water flow. Finally his principles also paved the way for futuristic advancements, like calculating rocket propulsion trajectories for space exploration (Enel Group, 2025). Each of these forms of innovation occurred because Isaac Newton saw what others had missed: Gravity wasn't a new invention; it required his unique ability to step back from individual observations and view them through a uniquely different lens.

Your ability to master a version of what Newton did, as you'll note throughout these pages, is at the core of becoming a changemaker: Even profound discoveries can be within reach if you learn to see differently, connect the dots, and act on the new insights this generates. Newton displayed the power of combining his simple yet disciplined thought process with deep personal curiosity proving out the universal truth—sometimes the solutions to the world's biggest challenges are not far off; they're just waiting for someone, anyone, to look closely enough to find them.

Another illustration of the groundbreaking solutions that can be discovered in this way happened in the early 1900s, long before the invention of refrigerators and modern preservation techniques emerged. Food contamination and spoilage were still life-threatening challenges at the time. Without a reliable way to keep food fresh, communities around the world faced severe health risks, from bacterial illnesses to widespread starvation. For generations, the inability to safely store and preserve food was simply accepted as an unavoidable reality. Yet, just like gravity, the solution to this global challenge existed right in front of everyone's eyes: heat.

In this example, it was the relentless curiosity and experimentation of Louis Pasteur that uncovered a profound connection between preservation and heat. In 1862, he demonstrated that heating wine to temperatures between 60 and 100 °C could kill off harmful microorganisms and prevent spoilage (Nelson, 2009). This simple yet revolutionary discovery revealed that food could be preserved—not just for days, but for months—by targeting the same bacteria responsible for its decay. Of course, Pasteur didn't invent heat, nor did he stumble upon a new technology. Rather, he applied the power of a familiar process in a way no one had thought to do previously.

Over the years, like Newton, Pasteur expanded on his insight, refined his method, and proved that the heating process could be used for a wide range of food products. That breakthrough laid the foundation for what we now know as pasteurization—a practice that went on to permanently transform food safety and revolutionize global food storage and transportation. Today, pasteurization is so ingrained in our everyday life that it's easy to forget how groundbreaking it once was. Pasteur was able to *see* a method for heating food that solved a problem plaguing humanity for centuries.

This example, like the one with Newton, illustrates how transformational change can occur by seeing the extraordinary in the ordinary. These breakthroughs weren't hidden in a lab or locked behind complex technology. They were outcomes of a simple, observable process waiting for someone with the curiosity and persistence to recognize their potential. In this way they also serve as real and powerful evidence of the core assumption made at the start of this chapter, that the answers to the biggest challenges may not be as distant or complicated as they seem, just waiting to be seen differently. These next examples aren't groundbreaking in the same ways Newton's and Pasteur's are, but of equal significance to this assumption:

A simple invention, used every day without a second thought, yet transformative in its own right, is the zipper. It's illuminating because the invention existed long before it was ever perfected. The first hints of the concept behind it can be traced back to the inventor of the sewing machine, Elias Howe, who first imagined it as a mechanism for fastening fabric. It was an enterprising Swede named Gideon Sundback who brought the design to life and made it practical (Bellis, 2016).

Like the others, the idea behind the zipper drew from principles that had existed for centuries before: The fundamental mechanism—interlocking teeth—was a staple of technology as far back as the second century BCE (Freeth, 2022). Gears with interlocking teeth were used, for example, to turn clock hands, power grain mills, and drive machinery. Howe saw the applications in everyday life and tapped their potential for fastening clothing. The idea was simple, visible, and already well understood—yet it wasn't fully realized until he took the step to reimagine its purpose.

It's now hard to imagine life without zippers. They're in our jackets, suitcases, shoes, and even high-tech gear like diving suits and spacesuits. What's more, despite its simplicity, the zipper has remained largely unchanged for over a century, demonstrating how effective a straightforward idea can be when applied in the right way. Once again, this seemingly small innovation solved a persistent problem with elegance and efficiency by leveraging a concept that had existed for hundreds of years.

The zipper is an innovation that grew from reimagining the familiar. Like the others, it illustrates that visionary ideas don't necessarily require groundbreaking technology or complex theories; sometimes they emerge from looking with fresh eyes. They give you a reason to reflect on your own ability to recognize untapped potential in the everyday, a skill that distinguishes changemakers.

This final example is one you can easily relate to in that a large and growing number of people use it daily without a second thought, and can help further stretch your thinking: contactless payment. Like the other examples, the technology behind this convenience isn't new. In fact, the foundation of contactless payments—near-field communication (NFC)—existed for decades before they became mainstream. The earliest form dates back to the 1940s, when radio wave frequencies were first harnessed for communication (Italy Magazine, 2024). Over time, the technology found practical uses in things like transit cards and access control systems, and finally made its way into our wallets and phones.

What makes the rise of contactless payment another compelling illustration is that its core technology—radio frequency identification—also existed for years, but it wasn't until the right combination of factors emerged—smartphones, upgraded point-of-sale (POS) terminals, and shifting consumer expectations on new ways to transact—that NFC's potential for fast, secure payments was fully realized. It took a unique alignment of infrastructure, technology, and demand to turn the long-standing technology into a global payment revolution.

The true tipping point that led to the mass use of contactless payments came with the global pandemic of 2020, which vastly accelerated the shift toward touch-free transactions. What had been a convenience suddenly became a necessity that's is now ubiquitous, with an estimated

2,372 transactions occurring every second (Radage, 2024). The technology's application now extends far beyond credit cards—we pay with our phones, smartwatches, rings, and even fingerprint-enabled biometric cards. In sum, what once seemed futuristic is now part of our daily routines, demonstrating how rapidly innovation can scale when the conditions are right.

The story of contactless payment is another example of reimagining existing technology to solve emerging problems. It demonstrates once again that changemaking doesn't necessarily require inventing something entirely new, if you can recognize how existing tools can be used in smarter, more impactful ways. It further substantiates the power of finding value in what's already around you and reshaping it to the needs of the moment.

Now it's time for you to take a step back and appreciate the bigger picture that these examples taken together reveal. Newton's discovery of gravity, Pasteur's breakthrough in food preservation, the invention of the zipper, and the widespread adoption of contactless payment, are part of a pattern: Persistent, creative thinking has the power to uncover new solutions by reimagining what exists, and harnessing this power creates the opportunity for you to tackle both big and small challenges. Remember, none of these breakthroughs were built from brand-new materials or undiscovered technologies; they emerged from an approach common to each of the examples provided that proves the potential exists to create impact that leads to something transformative.

To take these insights a step further, as you will see in the coming chapters this very same mindset may also apply to your personal ability to help solve today's greatest challenges. If rethinking something as simple as a zipper or harnessing an old technology like NFC can reshape industries, it's quite possible that the path to solving the most complex problems we face—climate change, economic justice, global conflict, and the like—might also be right in front of us. I recognize this may seem a bold leap to you. However, I'll illustrate that if you can implement the proper framework and adhere to the lessons learned, there's strong reason to believe difficult problems like these are not just addressable but potentially solvable.

To begin this part of your journey, there are three key elements for creating this capability and potential to effect change: focused attention, disciplined creativity, and the power of accelerating technology. As you've seen, having the ability to bring intense focus reveals patterns and opportunities that are easy to miss. In addition, creative and organized thinking allows you to connect insights in new ways. Finally, technology can redefine what's possible, and now at an astonishing rate. Taking the case of the enormous challenge we face in managing the changing climate as an example, technology has moved us far beyond pure observation to real-time monitoring, prediction, and even intervention. It shows that your ability to utilize the most advanced forms technology—which now includes AI, quantum computing, and other digital applications—has increased the potential for rapid innovation unlike anything we have seen before, opening doors that were firmly shut just a decade ago.

In fact, perhaps with some irony, you'll soon see that the biggest obstacles to solving the most challenging issues we face may actually not be technological at all. This is true because many of the solutions we need already exist. But also because an even tougher challenge is our ability to coordinate and collaborate with each other, at scale, collectively. In a world where the problems we face are often deeply connected, our ability to work together may determine our success more than any single invention. This is where the framework of the playbook you're developing takes on a significance and power all its own: Beyond uncovering hidden solutions, the ability to organize and amplify both individual and collective efforts to maximize the impact and change you can achieve.

Fortunately, as you will observe continually in the following chapters, the technologies that may actually be accelerating many of the problems we face today, like rapid changes in climate, can also help create the infrastructure that's essential to fostering global cooperation. Blockchain is a technology that is redefining trust and transparency, for example; artificial intelligence is optimizing decision-making; and real-time communication platforms are linking people across the world like never before. If used responsibly and effectively, these tools don't just help us spot hidden solutions—they help us build them together.

The road ahead is littered with challenges, but history shows that even the most deeply entrenched problems can often be solved using the right lens, the right mindset, and the right tools. And perhaps the most important insight that comes from all of these examples is that the solutions may actually already be in front of you—waiting for someone bold enough to bring them to light.

To fully set the stage I'll now share some of the most essential foundational elements of your playbook.

Coordination and Collaboration: The Heart of Widespread Change

You may wonder why I've placed the elements of coordination and collaboration front and center in your journey to become a changemaker. The answer is twofold: to understand it as a basic truth, and to recognize how crucial they are to accomplishing the most widespread impact and change possible. When I refer to coordination and collaboration, I specifically refer to the harmonization of efforts, resources, and talents required to achieve a shared goal. Like you observed in the previous section, history once again offers numerous examples that underscore the role that collective action plays in achieving unprecedented outcomes; evidence that when we combine our strengths and work together with a shared purpose, our total impact is greater than the sum of our individual efforts.

If you take another moment to think about some of the biggest issues we face—climate change, global poverty, food and water security, social equity—it's obvious that they are all complex and interconnected, demanding both innovative solutions and unprecedented collaboration across industry sectors, geographic borders, and generations. This makes it quite natural to wonder, "What can I do alone?" But history also teaches that the greatest progress is achieved when individuals amplify one another's efforts, exchange knowledge, and persevere together through setbacks. Indeed, some of the most impactful breakthroughs emerge from collective endeavors made up of diverse perspectives, fostering innovation, resilience, and hope. Working as a team leads to the generation of stronger ideas that can make our efforts more relentless, and our hope brighter. Every individual contribution matters, and every step forward builds momentum and fuels progress. In addition, collective action inspires greater confidence that change is actually possible if we refuse to give up personally, and keep pushing forward together. The following are eye-opening examples to reflect upon in this regard.

Take the eradication of the deadly disease of polio. It had plagued humanity for millennia—outbreaks were frequent and devastating, affecting children worldwide, leaving many dead or permanently disabled. By the mid-20th century, the disease had spread to every region of the globe, killing or paralyzing hundreds of thousands of children each year (Global Polio Eradication Initiative, 2023). In this respect, development of the inactivated polio vaccine by Professor Jonas Salk in the 1950s–1960s was a monumental breakthrough (Salk Institute for Biological Studies, 2015). However, it wasn't Salk alone who turned back polio—what made the difference was the massive mobilization of efforts by thousands of volunteers, health workers, scientists, and governments worldwide. It was a relentless combination of research, advocacy, and tireless work, coordinated across nations that represented the final push that brought polio to the brink of eradication. Ultimately, through this combination of efforts, polio cases were reduced by over 99 percent (World Health Organization, 2021).

This example of collaboration and extremely well-coordinated action is more than just a success story, though—it also shows the power that can come when mobilizing many individuals and groups, who each contribute their unique talents and perspectives, and how it can produce extraordinary results. It underscores the simple yet profound truth in focus: Major change very often requires collective effort—and the vital role that each of us can play, when working with perseverance and shared purpose. And the lesson goes beyond health. When individual activists, communities, organizations, and nations unite, it creates an opportunity to overcome seemingly impossible challenges. This is an encouraging reminder that hope is real and within our grasp when we join forces, and is fueled by action and cooperation.

There's also accepting the hard yet undeniable truth: Not trying is akin to giving up before the fight even begins. Making an effort offers the chance to learn, adapt, and eventually succeed; rather than remain blind to potential solutions, trapped by fear or doubt. Continuously trying, collaborating, and refining unlocks breakthroughs. The stories I've shared so far illustrate that breakthroughs aren't about instant success but about persisting in the face of setbacks. When fueled by hope, guided by resilience, and powered by collective effort, we turn daunting problems into opportunities for powerful change.

Notice that visionaries like Salk, Pasteur, and Newton didn't work alone—they relied on the support, ideas, and cooperation of many others. Their stories show that persistence and collaboration aren't just helpful—they're indispensable in turning overwhelming challenges into solutions that change lives. If you're a believer in the strength of working together, you also believe that the greatest obstacles are surmountable. It's this unstoppable combination of hope, effort, and unity that turns impossible dreams into tangible realities, and your personal playbook into a roadmap.

You'll learn in the chapters ahead how to build the kind of resilience and focus covered so far, and how to organize and amplify your efforts through a repeatable and flexible framework designed to achieve real impact. You'll also come to understand more clearly how determination and collaboration can unlock the full potential of our human ingenuity and personal intention. The solutions we need are actually not beyond our reach but waiting for us to work together and in tandem—doing so opens our eyes to new possibilities, and inspires us to keep pushing forward. You'll come to see a path to your own ability to help reimagine the world.

Dispelling the Myth of Impossibility

Laying the best foundation for the framework you'll use to implement your personal playbook starts with addressing perhaps the biggest mental barrier that can prevent you from taking action: the idea that "it's impossible."

I've learned from personal experience that one of the most effective ways to overcome feelings of doubt or reluctance is to break complex, intimidating problems into smaller, more manageable parts. At first glance, this might seem too simple—almost like a trick or an oversimplification. But stay with me, because this step is powerful. It helps you see that even the most daunting challenges aren't just one big, unbreakable wall—they are collections of smaller challenges, each of which can be tackled one step at a time. The truth is that when you break a problem down, it feels less overwhelming, and more within your reach—it clarifies what truly needs your attention, helps prioritize what you do first, and clears the way for steady progress. Most importantly, it shifts your mindset—changing your perception of the problem from an insurmountable mountain to a series of achievable tasks.

This extraordinary story in space exploration illustrates this mindset sharply. On April 17, 1970, NASA faced what seemed like the impossible—bringing home astronauts safely after a catastrophe on the Apollo 13 mission. Just 56 hours into their trip, an oxygen tank exploded, causing a fire and a catastrophic loss of power and life-support system. The situation quickly grew perilous. The crew was running out of oxygen—experts estimated only about an hour or two before it would be too late for them.

NASA's flight director, Eugene Kranz, didn't panic. Instead, he and his team focused carefully on what was most critical: how to keep the astronauts alive longer and find a way to bring them safely back to Earth. They broke the crisis into its core parts—how to fix the oxygen problem, conserve power, and manage reentry. They didn't try to fix everything all at once. Instead, they pinpointed the most urgent issues and tackled them one by one. Using whatever materials they had on board—plastic covers, duct tape, lithium hydroxide capsules—they crafted a makeshift filter for the carbon dioxide, which was suffocating the crew. Then they devised a new reentry plan, even jettisoning the heavy service module to make the capsule lighter and better control their descent into Earth's atmosphere.

It was an extraordinary challenge, and the lead engineer once admitted that their chances of success were "slim to none." Yet, through calm focus, disciplined teamwork, resourcefulness, and relentless perseverance, NASA's engineers and astronauts worked together seamlessly—breaking each problem into smaller parts, zeroing in on what mattered most, and improvising with what they had.

This story is a forceful reminder that focusing on the core issues, and handling each one piece by piece, can turn even the most impossible challenges into successes. It's about training your mind to stay calm and organized under pressure, trusting in your skills, and refusing to accept defeat. With patience, resilience, and a firm belief that solutions are within your reach—no matter how tough the situation—you can accomplish remarkable things. Because almost anything truly is possible if you approach it in this way, with determination and a teamwork mindset to guide you forward.

Building Our House: Looking Ahead

The coming chapters draw on inspiring examples, like the Apollo 13 mission, to show just how much you can accomplish with a disciplined yet flexible perspective—and you approach even the biggest challenges with a mindset that says, "It's possible." Seeing these real-world stories will help ease the hesitation or doubt you might feel about taking action yourself. Remember, if others can turn the seemingly impossible into success, so can you.

As you walk through these examples, I also introduce practical tools designed to help you reimagine the type and amount of impact you're capable of achieving. You'll begin to notice as well, and fairly quickly, that a changemaker playbook can't be complete without acknowledging the versatile and all-important role that the most modern technologies play in today's world. Whether it's used to simplify processes, accelerate action, or automate efforts, the constantly evolving tech landscape has become a vital partner—an extension of your own drive and vision. It allows you to tackle more complex problems than ever before, expanding your reach, increasing your speed, and amplifying your impact, every day.

I also dedicate a whole chapter in Part IV to the art and science of collaboration. You'll see how working effectively with others—especially across different skills, resources, and networks—has become an ever-more-exciting and vital skill. You'll also explore the role and potential of "super networks"—expansive webs of people and data that grow stronger with every connection—and learn how these networks fuel what's called a "network effect," capable of magnifying our collective effort exponentially. The internet is constantly fomenting the creation and expansion of these vast, rapid-fire "super networks" that connect individuals and organizations around the globe, sparking innovation and opening doors to impact that were once unimaginable. When knowledge spreads quickly and influence multiplies across these networks, it brings a whole new dimension to how our combined efforts can stir remarkable change—far more than any single person or small group could achieve alone.

I emphasize that the greatest potential for impact lies in uniting our efforts—thinking differently about how we mobilize. Achieving the kind of coordinated action needed to carry out your plan requires a shift in your own mindset—a kind of "retraining" of the way you see yourself and your role. Luckily, this shift is already happening around us—social media, in particular, is a powerful example. You'll explore how the evolving relationship with these platforms is reshaping how we think, communicate, and act. When used thoughtfully and intentionally for good, social media can mobilize masses, create momentum, and amplify your efforts.

Chapter 10 goes deeper into harnessing the potential of social media—showing how to combine it with other groundbreaking technologies to build impactful momentum, especially when each action is rooted in purpose and strategy. The possibilities for a changemaker to integrate seamlessly with the tools at our fingertips, are making our collective impact more dynamic and achievable.

Finally, remember that technology alone is not enough. The true power lies in our personal commitment—your "will" to push through doubts, setbacks, and the inevitable obstacles that arise in any change journey. Your personal strength will determine how far your efforts go. When you combine this inner resilience with the external tools, networks, and strategies, you become unstoppable.

As you approach the final chapters of this journey, a clear and repeatable path will emerge—one that shows how individual effort and collective action together can drive real, lasting change in many different situations. Big change isn't just a distant dream—it's a tangible reality you can help shape. The tools and strategies are within your grasp, waiting for you to harness them with purpose. And with an unrelenting commitment to keep moving forward—step by step—you can create a lasting impact that ripples far beyond your own efforts.

Now, let's get started on building your changemaker's playbook. The future is waiting—let's go create it, one action at a time.

2 | Clearing Fatal Roadblocks and Avoiding the Paralysis of Complexity

Welcome to your first—and arguably most essential—step toward creating meaningful change: truly believing that it's possible.

In the previous chapter, I emphasized the importance of recognizing opportunities in plain sight and taking that first bold step forward. But before you can convert creative thinking into action, you must confront a fundamental barrier many of us face: the fear that problems are simply too vast, too complex, or too overwhelming to overcome. It's perfectly natural to feel this way. When you stand at the base of a mountain and look up, the climb can seem insurmountable, even impossible. It's easy to doubt whether you have what it takes to make a difference, or to dismiss your potential entirely before you even begin.

If this sounds familiar, keep reading. The key isn't to avoid attempting solutions because the problems seems too difficult; as touched upon in the first chapter, it's to learn how to break down large, intimidating problems into smaller, more manageable parts. Over time, you find that when you focus on each one individually, those daunting mountains become a series of achievable milestones.

Chapter 2 grounds this idea with some real examples—stories from my own experience to help you adapt toward this mindset, and show how breaking problems down clears the path, even when you feel stuck.

Whenever I confront a complex challenge, I start, exactly in this way, by deconstructing it. After many years in change management, I've repeatedly seen that this approach not only leads to a clearer understanding of the core issues but also reveals more effective solutions. Just as importantly, I found that the changes we succeed in putting into place stoke your momentum and self-confidence, creating a ripple effect that sparks even larger break-throughs over time.

No matter how daunting your challenge might seem, breaking it into manageable steps naturally reveals opportunities and reminds you that you are capable of making meaningful change, as you go. The more you practice breaking problems down, the stronger your confidence and resilience become—arming you to face larger challenges with clarity, purpose, and a strategic mindset.

First Insights: Breaking It Down

The next section starts with a simple example that's fairly easy to understand, even if you're unfamiliar with the business world. A common problem faced by large consumer-facing companies—banks for instance—is how a poor customer experience with one product or service can impact the entire company's performance. Investigating the underlying causes of the customer experience is essential in a situation like this, both to pinpoint the problem and to determine how best to fix it. The path to doing so consistently involves building a *bottom-up* understanding, which on the surface can feel a little intimidating. Don't worry, I'll walk you through how it's applied, one step at a time.

bottom-up understanding, n.: An understanding achieved by analyzing an issue from the ground level—by looking at specific data points, experiences, or root causes—before drawing broader conclusions or developing solutions.

I begin by giving you a sense of the scope and complexity of solving a problem like the one shown in Figure 2.1. The steps to be taken in situations like this often translate into building a basic understanding of many hundreds of individual product and service offerings, across dozens of different businesses and customer types.

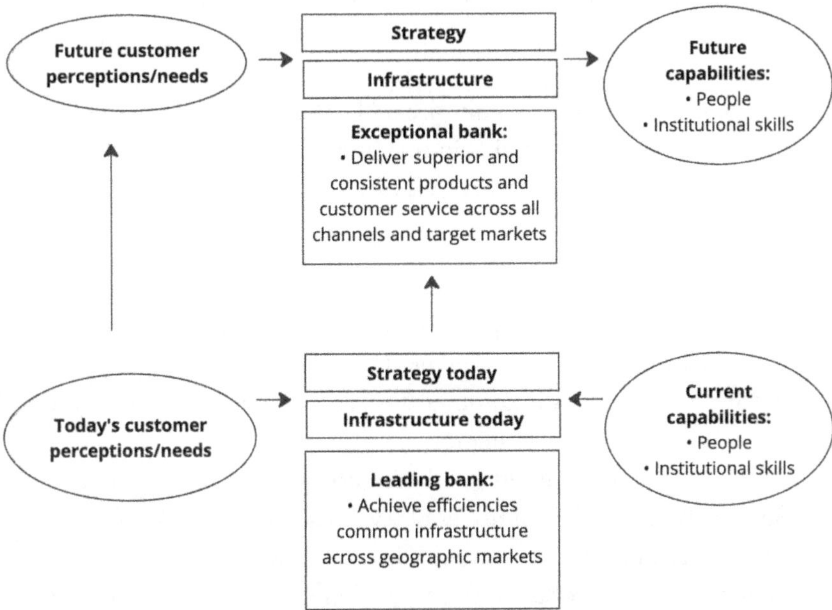

Figure 2.1　Transformation of business infrastructure to enable your strategies: comparing current with future state.

Despite the various considerations, you find over time that there is a remarkable consistency to the questions that need to be asked across them, that initially seem quite different on the surface (e.g., the customer experience of a small business versus one pursuing a home mortgage loan). Building an understanding of how, where, and why issues arise ironically comes down to a relatively common set of questions and considerations. In my experiences these three would always sit right at the center of developing that understanding:

- First, what are the ways that a customer physically or virtually encounters your product or service currently—advertising, promotion, in-store purchase, office or branch visit, phone, chat, or online?
- Next, where do each of these encounters begin to break down—become more difficult, complicated, inconvenient, unpleasant, or unreliable for a customer?
- Then, what would the ideal experience be as compared to what customers were currently experiencing in each of these types of encounters?

The approach thus is to continually probe further, step by step, to identify the practical considerations and adjustments that will lead to a better overall experience for the customer. Figure 2.2 provides an illustration of this approach.

1. Understand current infrastructure, process, and strategy for retention measurement and tracking, cross sales, customer servicing and customer information management.
2. Evaluate root cause of customer dissatisfaction from exit surveys and historical customer information.
3. Work in conjunction with marketing to analyze MCIF system, or similar database, at the household level (e.g., top decile profitability analysis/product mix) or account level, if possible.
4. Identify current product offering (including strength and weakness analysis) with product management and also provide best-of-breed products in market.
5. Evaluate current problem resolution protocol from identification to resolution response.
6. Perform rigorous assumption testing of recommended in overall design (with DCT, marketing, legal, etc.).
7. Refine model with strategic input from top management.
8. Outline detailed implementation plan.

Figure 2.2 Theme validation: customer satisfaction and loyalty.

The process of breaking problems by asking key questions like these makes the effort to understand their causes more manageable, focused, and actionable; Figure 2.2 is also useful for demonstrating how complicated challenges like this are tackled—one step at a time, with clarity and purpose—zeroing in on the primary issues.

Figure 2.3 is a continuation of the work displayed in the previous figure that shows how the thoughts that these questions generate are iteratively refined to highlight the differences.

Gaps between operational infrastructure and strategic goals established

Identified Gaps
- Call center technology does not allow for full integration of phone and web-based response to customer inquiries.
- Customer surveys reveal inconsistent practices when interacting with the branch, phone, and internet to fulfill sales needs leading to higher abandonment rates. Branch and customer service center agents have access to different customer information.
- Some customer service phone calls go to branch staff (as opposed to the direct customer service center), leaving branch staff with less time to sell. Individual branch phone numbers are currently listed on the website.

Hypotheses
- Customer confusion is caused by inconsistent sales and service practices across different delivery channels.
- Branch staff's ability to maximize sales efforts is hampered by routine customer service inquiries.

Emerging redesign theme
- Upgrade call center technology to more efficiently handle customer inquiries through multiple communication channels and focus branch platform staff on sales challenges by removing call volume and providing improved customer information.

Themes and ideas developed

Approved theme

Create consistent sales and service processes for all delivery channels by providing common customer information for branch and customer service center agents, rerouting inquiries to an enhanced VRU, and integrating voice/web-based sales and service delivery.

Ideas

- Consider innovative multimedia contact center solutions that include web-based solutions such as text chat and email response in addition to the traditional IVR.
- Provide branch and multimedia contact center agents with online access to common customer information to maximize sales and service effectiveness and ensure a positive customer experience.
- Consolidate rerouting of calls and migrate customers to web-based response units at the customer's preference.

Benefits

- Increase customer satisfaction by handling sales and service, reducing wait time, and increasing customer and staff satisfaction.
- Enable branch staff to focus on in-person sales and service.

Figure 2.3   Gap analysis leads to future state development.

Source: Branch network/direct distribution channels

Moving Forward: Revealing a Path to Action

Figures 2.4 and 2.5 illustrate how the common threads identified in the previous section began to inform a completely new operational design for delivering the company's products and services. To review, the first step broke down the problem: the negative impact that customers' poor experiences with products and services were having on the company; a set of questions were then asked to build a better understanding of the underlying causes of the experiences. Over time, we found that applying this common approach (shaped here and there to reflect any truly unique characteristics) uncovered the root of the problem across many different products and services. This of course has an obvious way of reducing the complexity one originally perceives at the outset, and a natural way of revealing how to address a shared problem with a common solution. Figure 2.4 represents an early output reflecting this process.

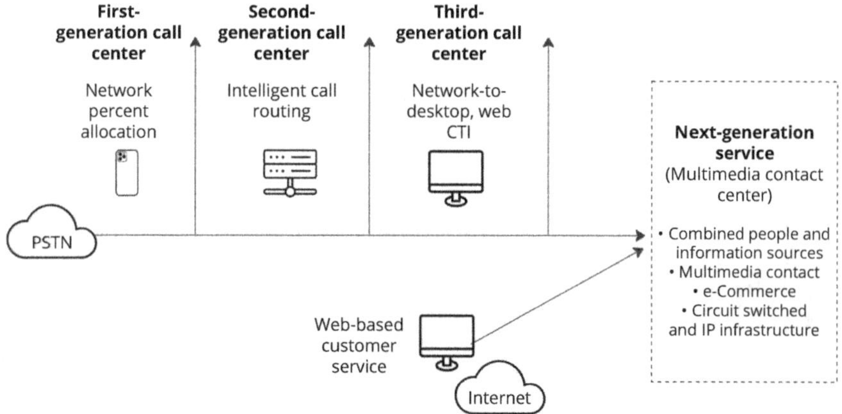

Figure 2.4   Theme building blocks and evolution of customer contact to achieve future state.

It's helpful to take note that personal experiences like the one shared here are just one part of overhauling a company's overall operating efficiency. I mention this because it helps put the magnitude of these situations into perspective—they seem enormous and challenging, and are, but far from impossible. It does and always will take time, to be sure; and has to be done in a thoughtful and thorough way. However, having personally applied the approach in this example many times, I discovered that it consistently reveals a similar type of insight and a corresponding route to actions with the highest priority; this, as mentioned, despite the unique aspects existing within different departments, brands, geographies, and so on. Let me give you a better sense of what I mean.

Stepping Back

For further context, when all of the activities, skills, and tools that a business requires to achieve optimal performance are both in place and operating in a seamless and well-coordinated manner, the business is considered operationally efficient.

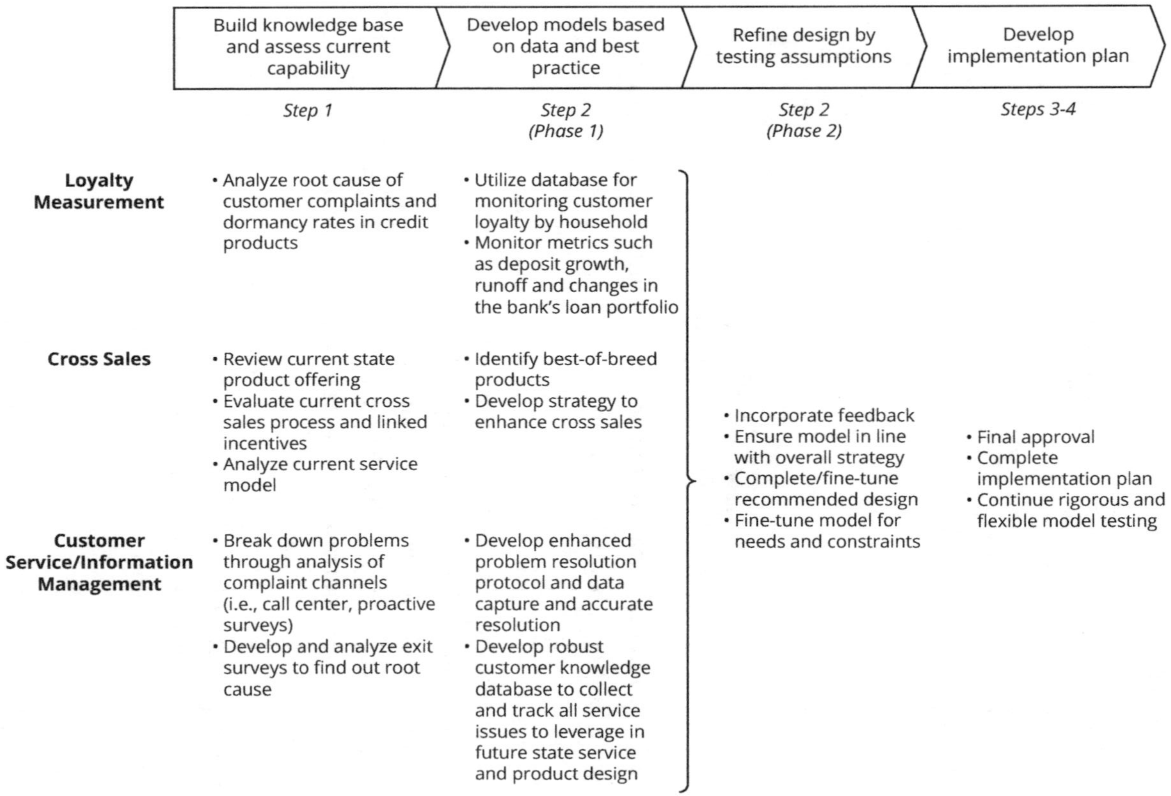

Build knowledge base and assess current capability	Develop models based on data and best practice	Refine design by testing assumptions	Develop implementation plan
Step 1	*Step 2 (Phase 1)*	*Step 2 (Phase 2)*	*Steps 3-4*

Loyalty Measurement	• Analyze root cause of customer complaints and dormancy rates in credit products	• Utilize database for monitoring customer loyalty by household • Monitor metrics such as deposit growth, runoff and changes in the bank's loan portfolio		
Cross Sales	• Review current state product offering • Evaluate current cross sales process and linked incentives • Analyze current service model	• Identify best-of-breed products • Develop strategy to enhance cross sales	• Incorporate feedback • Ensure model in line with overall strategy • Complete/fine-tune recommended design • Fine-tune model for needs and constraints	• Final approval • Complete implementation plan • Continue rigorous and flexible model testing
Customer Service/Information Management	• Break down problems through analysis of complaint channels (i.e., call center, proactive surveys) • Develop and analyze exit surveys to find out root cause	• Develop enhanced problem resolution protocol and data capture and accurate resolution • Develop robust customer knowledge database to collect and track all service issues to leverage in future state service and product design		

Figure 2.5   Enhancing customer expression and loyalty.

It is no small task for a company to achieve the highest operational efficiency possible. Just like our service example, it means gaining a basic yet full understanding of the company's current business activities, and identifying the root cause of any inefficiencies that exist across different areas of the company. The issues uncovered by this approach can of course be happening for a whole host of reasons. Perhaps business roles (or the work processes that staff engage in) are being completely duplicated elsewhere in the company, or there is a redundant use of a particular technical system or tool, overly complicated procedures are being used, and so on. The goal is to spot these and other major bottlenecks that are affecting the speed, effectiveness, and overall coordination of business activities across the entire organization.

In each case, this involves improving the efficiency of an individual business or total company by examining the roles and responsibilities in each area that touch some part of the customer experience. By breaking down activities and workflows, major opportunities begin to present themselves—most typically ones that can streamline, standardize, or otherwise simplify the way these activities are taking place.

Figure 2.6 shows how each area of a business is broken down into the particular functions they supply to the company—which, incidentally, also tends to be surprisingly consistent not just within but across industries! They include general business management, human resources, finance, product and service areas, technology and operations, and many more. For each line of business, every product or service is further broken down into the core activities involved in delivering it to the customer. Every area is then reviewed to identify gaps in the skills needed to perform a particular business role or activity; where the activities supporting one area might depend unnecessarily on the involvement of others in the organization; or where insufficient attention is being paid to essential activities, due to limitations in the amount—or type—of resource that is needed, for example.

In parallel, look for the ways it might be possible to simplify and/or automate current work steps. These actions were taken across hundreds of individual workflows; the insights generated were then compared to best practices and standard performance and efficiency benchmarks for the industry, always with the goal to spot the major gaps and differences between the two.

Redesign team	Process groups
Investments	• Investments under advice • Investments under administration • Investments under management
Branch division	• Metropolitan branch network • State and territory branch network
Electronic/direct	• Operations • Direct banking • Electronic banking
Mortgage/consumer lending	• Network mortgage lending • Personal consumer lending • Third party mortgage origination • Mortgage operations/securities • Consumer and commercial collections/ recovery
Commercial	• Treasury • Risk management • Automotive finance • Business banking • Corporate banking
Information technology	• IT development • IT production
Support services	• Facilities • Finance • HR • Marketing/Communications
Cross corporate	• Purchasing • Policy

Figure 2.6   Future state redesign components.

And from there, we moved on to the following: First, assess the relative difficulty of the actions that would need to be taken to address each identified gap, and prioritize what to attack first; once again assessing the skills, resources, and tools required to carry them out effectively. From there, develop ways to monitor progress in each area and understand the combined impact of changes implemented across the company in total!

Remarkably, time and time again, I saw the promise of using this same set of steps to collect insights and take impactful action across numerous areas despite unique variables, in a manageable and highly organized way. This is a central theme throughout the book: Regardless of a problem's size or nature, a practical and logical approach will allow you to identify what the areas affecting customers have in common, and to generate plenty of opportunities to take meaningful action.

Of note, the steps may differ somewhat depending on whether you are focused *outwardly* on the customers' perception of product or service quality, or *inwardly* on how well a company is actually structured to operate internally. Where this holds true, the steps are adjusted to account for the truly unique differences between the two, but in large part all can be approached using the same basic process.

The strength of using a structured, yet flexible, set of steps like this in order to frame the way you think about and tackle issues isn't limited to untangling and solving business problems, either. You can also apply them to much smaller challenges as well.

Breaking Down the Day-to-Day

The ability to apply this thinking universally can be seen in our business as well as personal lives: the good sense of keeping what we spend in line with what we earn provides a great example in this regard. Interestingly, a similar set of steps to those taken in the banking case can also be used to gain better clarity on the ways that we, consciously or otherwise, run our own business or personal life, and leads us toward setting better priorities and making better, more informed choices on the amount we spend, as well as how/where/when we decide to spend it.

You can ask the following set of analogous questions to build perspective on needed changes, set new goals, prioritize your actions, and ready yourself to make the changes needed to balance your budget:

- What are the biggest sources of income received (cash in) in and expenditures made (cash out)?
- Where do they come from (i.e., how are they generated)?
- Are there other potential sources of income to collect that you have not accounted for?
- Where are the "out-of-pocket" expenses discretionary versus unavoidable?
- Can expenditures be reduced or entirely cut by changing what you do or how you do them?
- Can you adjust the timing of what you spend to better preserve the cash you have on hand?

While reflecting on these questions, take the very same steps as those demonstrated in the banking example:

1. Decide the basis you will use for prioritizing the actions you will take—to adjust your spending and address the gap between what you make and what you spend.
2. Establish the action steps you will commit to. For example, to find an online resource or other tool to help you reduce and generally help keep better track of expenditures, and to strengthen your spending discipline.
3. Finally, take action on what you prioritize and track your progress, staying flexible to needed adjustments to your plan along the way.

The pattern among these different examples becomes even clearer when you compare them. Each was approached using a similar set of practical questions in order to better understand the problems to be solved. This was accomplished by identifying and reflecting on their main causes, assessing the actions you thought might best address them, and adjusting the plan as you observe the effects that result from them.

Now notice that an overall template is beginning to emerge, one that you can use broadly and effectively in both simple and complex situations alike, and that yields remarkable consistency in both the success you can have in the actions you take *as well as* the total impact they achieve. Despite the simplicity and intuitiveness of the steps you've been introduced to in this chapter, the next section gives you an even further sense of their broad utility by showing how they generally apply to much larger issues—even ones with the potential for global impact.

Complex Questions: A First Look

This section illustrates the universal nature of the approach I've shared by looking at the common threads between the previously reviewed examples and ones with the potential impact that stretches far beyond them. Think about asking questions like these as baby steps toward building your capacity and confidence to drive personal impact with the potential to help change the world. This section outlines a number of examples, that are of that scale and pivotal to sustaining life. Note how they follow the playbook of breaking them down into their component parts in order to spur ideas on how to approach them.

Climate: Reducing Greenhouse Gas Emissions

We can ask:

- What are the major things that cause these emissions and how are they generated?
- What are the changes to human behavior that can decrease them?
- What are the alternative and renewable sources that can replace them?
- What are the biggest stumbling blocks for increasing the use of alternative and renewable energy sources, both at a personal level and commercially?
- How can we become more effective at improving energy efficiency, personally and in our businesses?
- What are the main ways we can electrify industries and better promote sustainable land use?
- What prevents us from doing so on a global level?

Health: Becoming Better Prepared for a Public Health Crisis

We can begin by asking:

- How can we design better processes and mechanisms for developing and distributing effective vaccines?
- What are the main changes that must occur in order to enhance public health infrastructure and surveillance?
- What are the main ways to promote global cooperation and information sharing?

Food: Achieving Global Food Security

We can start to understand the path by asking:

- What are the main technologies and inventions that can increase agricultural productivity and sustainable farming practices on a global scale?
- What access to tools, guides, and partnerships already exist, or can be created to support small-scale farmers and local food systems?
- What is blocking huge agricultural companies from modifying the current system? What parts can be feasibly replaced or modified?
- What are the main factors currently blocking improvement in food distribution and waste reduction systems?

Water: Protecting Marine Biodiversity

A thoughtful reflection on how we can individually impact this issue would include answering questions like these:

- Where are the threats to biodiversity the biggest?
- What are the major causes of the threat?
- How do they compare in different regions of the world? Are there common reasons for them?
- What must be in place to sufficiently protect marine areas and sanctuaries?
- What practices and policies exist or do we need to further adopt to reduce causes, such as plastic pollution and industrial waste?
- How can we better promote sustainable fishing and aquaculture practices?

Key Takeaways

After walking through the range of different challenges summarized, the main insight is this: There are always simple, logical steps you can take to think more clearly about the challenges you take on. Whether it's in your personal life, in business, or at a world level—your chances of driving impact will increase as you continue to ask questions that provide an opportunity to reflect on them at a lower level, and think more deeply about the problem at hand. Steps like the ones reviewed help you organize your thoughts and prevent you from feeling paralyzed by complexity.

Is it too much to believe that breaking down challenges on a smaller scale might also help get to the root of solving massive ones, like the worrying effects of climate change? Is it truly realistic to think that we can discover new pathways and solutions that might be lying in plain sight? Or are these possibilities still too hard for you to imagine?

Examples like the ones covered thus far and many others like them suggest strongly that attacking long-standing problems in this way can be an exciting new source of needed change. That said, these outcomes won't be achieved without something equally essential: making a successful transition from deep, creative thinking to disciplined, deliberate action. This shift in focus is the critical path for changing your perception of the difficulty attached to reaching your goal to actually achieving it.

You will feel increasingly well-armed on how to make this shift as we progress through subsequent chapters; I will also share a first-hand experience that illustrates how you can translate your newly found confidence into having an impact on gargantuan things like global poverty. Indeed, while dramatically and distinctly different on the surface, you will begin notice that what they share in common represents an exciting gateway to unimagined progress.

Chapter 3 builds on this premise by delving into another essential element of your changemaker's playbook: *solving problems and creating new realities rests on a well-defined process.*

The Framework

Part II picks up where Part I left off by building on the foundational thinking put forth in the first two chapters. It looks at the remarkable results that can occur when you ask a standard set of questions to confront most any challenge.

- Chapter 3 speaks to the importance of a consistent and disciplined approach, and the confidence we reinforce within by utilizing a structured yet versatile "changemaker playbook process" to help reimagine the future.

- Chapter 4 illustrates the success that comes from consistently applying the process laid out in the previous chapter, while also infusing flexibility into the plans we implement to account for inevitable adjustments that will be needed over time. The essential role of flexibility is also brought to life with a real story of using the process both to create a solution and to re-create it when the environment completely shifted.

3

The Power of Process in a Changemaker's Practice

In the chapter ahead I expand on the fundamental principles of becoming a changemaker shared so far, by asking you to reflect on them as you would approach building a new home. Part I helps you create the foundation for the structure, and Part II will help you build its frame. By the end, using the references and illustrations I provide as a guide, you will begin to feel your ability to create your own personal playbook begin to take shape—like a home complete with insulation, walls, and a roof—and you will have a strong and sturdy structure for taking action with impact. You will also observe how concepts that at first seem difficult to apply practically at first become progressively less so, and, as subsequent chapters get more and more specific, you will observe the playbook come together piece by piece.

> *process,* n.: A deliberate, step-by-step approach to building something meaningful—like constructing a house, one piece at a time, with each phase depending on the strength and clarity of the last. A series of steps with a dedicated goal or desired outcome.

It's time to get underway, but don't worry—I guide you through it gradually, beginning with a recap of key insights from earlier chapters.

First, as I noted at the very start, really big problems are indeed hard to solve, given the numerous individual considerations and pieces that must magically come together in order to achieve a planned outcome. It's not just true, its also completely logical, making it far easier to focus on the things in life we feel we have the most control over. Simply put, our personal world feels more manageable when we stay focused on our day-to-day accomplishments. But as the real situations I've shared with you thus far also show, some of the challenges that seem either too big or too complicated to take on (let alone fix) at the outset are not only solvable, but also surmountable—and manageable, too. That truth is the rock I build upon in this next chapter.

As you'll soon see, the impossible can suddenly seem doable, and your ability to successfully solve difficult challenges becomes an exciting new prospect! Indeed, the inspiration you begin to feel may have you recognizing for the first time your own potential to change your business, your life, perhaps even the world. Believe it or not, this is exactly what happened to me. I'll share epiphanies I received during my own journey in changemaking with you now, and give you an idea of how it can work for you, too. So let's dive back in and have a look at some of the things that have been part of my personal practice for years now, and proven successful in a wide variety of situations.

Steps for Success

To begin, as reviewed last chapter, asking a series of straightforward questions is a "go-to" way to organize your thoughts when confronting a complex challenge; in this section, I'll now cover key steps that help you organize your *actions*.

As explained in Chapter 2, getting bogged down by a problem's size or complexity is, without a doubt, the arch enemy of creativity and progress. It can block you mentally from venturing toward taking any action at all, but consider the following to understand why it doesn't have to. As you saw with the pattern that emerged from the examples I've shared, there is always an opportunity to break down challenges in order to understand them on a deeper level. And doing so can also help you to discover the self-confidence to forge on. As simple as this may now sound, it was a real revelation for this changemaker that has reinforced itself over and over again, and is now a fundamental building block of the changemaker's playbook you will build.

Let's now turn to something just as crucial to this ready-set-go approach: how the steps I outlined in the last chapter come together to form a repeatable process you can consistently use to drive real and lasting change. Just as in the previous situations, I'll give you a better idea of how this works in practice. There are four main steps to the process, which can be concisely summed up:

- **Current versus future state analysis:** Assess differences between how things are currently occurring and how they would work in an ideal scenario.
- **Gap analysis:** Brainstorm answers to the question "What's the fix?" Identify ways to augment or replace parts of certain workflows, add a new tool, a role, or a technical solution.
- **Set the plan:** Identify actions to implement, order to proceed, based on best potential.
- **Refinement cycle:** Observe, learn, refine, and *repeat.*

Turning Process into Practice

Here's what I know about the possibilities for you to take action with impact and to deliver change: A well-defined and organized process allows you to both navigate the most critical paths for effecting change and to consider your potential for impact at every stage. A process helps you prevent important pieces of the plans you create from falling through the cracks. Having said this, you must keep in mind that it is just as critical that you not confuse a *well-defined* process with one that is inflexible or overly complicated.

The approach NASA took in the Apollo 13 crisis discussed in Chapter 1 helps to illustrate this important distinction. Believe it or not, you can see evidence of utilizing these steps for finding a solution to the grave circumstances faced on board. NASA's plan for bringing the astronauts back safely ultimately worked, in large part, because of the team's supreme ability to rapidly incorporate new information as it surfaced and new events as they unfolded. The actions they took to dynamically adjust to the continuously changing circumstances onboard the capsule were imperative to the success they ultimately had in safely returning the astronauts back to Earth. This involved, in part, continuously engaging in a *gap analysis,* by combining careful observation with the question "What's the fix?" From there they were able to set a plan, and then continuously refine it as new factors arose.

Notice, also, in the NASA example that while precision was indeed mission-critical in many ways, their decisions by definition could not be, given the number of variables and unknowns. It was a situation with zero room for error, but also where the ability to be totally accurate was greatly obstructed. It's a wonderful example of one of the cardinal rules of the changemaker's playbook, and in life, regarding the myth of perfection: using the 80:20 rule as your guide for deciding what actions to take.

80:20 rule, idiom: A principle stating that 80 percent of the outcome for a given event is a result of 20 percent of the input.

Aiming for an 80 versus 100 percent confidence level that a solution will be effective can dramatically increase your likelihood for success. Let me explain why. It may seem obvious, but a process that is successful in solving a problem must have at its core a "working" assumption on what it means to solve it—that is, how the situation will differ and what it will look like when it is finally solved. In short, developing a set of initial assumptions, or hypotheses, helps you think more clearly about the steps needed to achieve your goals. Do so by looking at the specifics of the situation at hand, alongside what an ideal outcome might look like. Think of it as a side-by-side comparison: that is, things are like this now, but ideally they would be that way—by clearing this roadblock, preventing that consequence, and so on. I continually refer to this piece of your playbook as the *current versus future state comparison,* using the following basic definitions:

current state, n.: The present circumstances; the situation as it is now.

▌*future state,* n.: The situation as it would be in an ideal future scenario.

Here's an example from my personal experience of how this comparison becomes central to changemaking. For context, my journey with changemaking began right out of school in the financial industry, where I spent about 15 years or so—first learning the ropes, then guiding major corporations—through a specific process designed to address business problems that were preventing them from reaching their stated strategic, financial, operational, technological, and managerial goals.

Each of these situations was without exception highly complex, with many difficult issues to address, scattered across different businesses, product lines, and operational functions. They all also had conflicting and overlapping parts. As a result, improving on an issue in one of these areas would often have a negative effect somewhere else in the company, sometimes multiple other areas. It is where I first learned (at times the hard way) the importance that the process I pass on to you in this chapter carries, and the role that comparing the current to the future state plays for ensuring that existing linkages and overlaps across different businesses, products, and so on are as clear as possible before trying to identify feasible solutions. Let's return to the customer experience example discussed last chapter to get a practical idea of how it was used.

Recall in Chapter 2 that I broke down a broad problem of customers' poor experience with a company's product in order to understand why it existed, as a quick reference I began by answering these questions:

- What are the ways a customer currently encounters your product—advertising, promotion, in-store, phone, online?
- Where does their experience break down in each of these types of encounters?
- What would the experience ideally look and feel like?

After asking these questions, the next step was to explore the differences more deeply by looking at the ways the customer encounters these products and services now:

- Product or service inquiries and customer service—including in-person, phone, and virtual online assistant.

Where the experience they have begins to break down:

- The current customer service experience varies depending on how and where it takes place, and the inconsistent quality of service across them reflects this.
- The answers received due to a service representatives' ability to resolve issues can vary substantially, when addressed in person versus virtual assistant versus online.
- The technical and operating systems supporting each type and location of service vary substantially—for example, the virtual assistant may be using a combination of existing customer data and AI-generated responses, while a live representative may have access only to product order information.

The specific details of the situation, of course, increased as I focused on how, when, and where the customer's experience actually begins to break down.

Creating a better experience required comparing the details gathered on the service customers were receiving in their various encounters (the *current state*) to what they can look forward to once the issues are solved (the *future state*). We considered what the new experience would ideally be like:

- One consistent, seamless experience, regardless of how we choose to encounter.
- The systems issues impacting the experience are solved through management, technology, or process changes that are needed.

What you might begin to notice is that each of these steps is part of a methodical *process* that allows you to identify the issues at hand, and develop a rationale on how to change them. While it will never make a perfect solution to any problem magically appear, it represents an extremely helpful and practical template for evaluating fixes. Time and time again, it demonstrates that simply writing your thoughts down on paper, on a sticky note, or on a whiteboard can lead you toward sharper working assumptions, and avenues for experimentation. Now you might be thinking, "Okay, great—so far.

I now know how this process will lead me to ask important questions about the problem I want to solve, and how to start creating some initial ideas…but where does the action come in, and more importantly, the confidence that I can be successful?"

These are the logical and correct questions to ask, as even in a relatively simple illustration, the range of considerations needed to move from the current to the future state can feel overwhelming at times, especially when taking into account the variety of people, roles, work areas, resources, and costs. In addition, as previously pointed out and has been consistently true in my own experiences, there are often also interdependencies across different businesses and product lines, as well as in the operational functions that support them, that further add to the complexity.

In every situation, however, I found that most of these factors could be meaningfully addressed by delving into the current state of a product or business, not just in isolation but across them, from how products are developed and marketed, all the way through to how they are delivered to the customer (for purposes of the playbook I refer to this as building and "end-to-end" perspective)—and in almost every instance it was also often the case that many of the important things needed to reach the future state were not unlike our examples in Chapter 1, right there in plain sight.

end-to-end, adj.: From the very beginning of a process to the very end.

The process I'm sharing reinforces one of the basic truths I touched on earlier and bears repeating: Perfection in anything is a myth. If we're being realistic, we know that we can't expect our experiences in life to be perfect. This leads to another cardinal rule of the playbook: In business as in life, the goal must be to prioritize the decisions and actions you believe can get you as close as possible to reaching your goals. The customer experience illustration shows how the process shared with you in this chapter is used to align a company's perception of its product and service quality with what can be understood about the customer's expectations, and to identify actions that can reduce the gaps between the two—things like improved responsiveness, increased accuracy, thorough answers to questions, and a pleasant exchange were very often chief among them.

Keeping the current versus future state construct at the center of our thoughts—and noting the differences between the two that prompt you to ask *why*—leads to identify what's missing:

- Why is the service different when accessed in a store rather than by phone or online?
- Why is the service level of lower quality when we seek it in person in one location versus another?
- Why are the answers to questions slower to be received, not complete, or not accurate?

Asking *why*, then, is what allows us to spot issues lying at the root of the problem, and uncover the disconnects that exist between what customers may consider ideal and the way things are currently designed.

A clear example of this emerges when you look at the differing sets of technical capabilities needed to support the customer's experience depending on where and how they encounter it, such as by phone, virtual assistant, or some other form of automated service. For example, customer service representatives can be accessing completely different technical platforms that have very few capabilities in common. As a result, their access to the customer information and tools to address issues also differ. Like previous illustrations, the situation at first blush begins to feel too complicated to try and address, but in fact many if not most of these issues are solved to customers' satisfaction by simply identifying where systems need to work better together to achieve greater consistency, and then to build the appropriate connections across them.

Again, focusing on the differences between the current and future state, specifically the gaps between the two, often reveals the most natural paths to fixing them. In fact, just like Newton, you'll discover that the situation has never been looked at in that particular way before, causing solutions to simply fall between the cracks.

Reframing and Refining

The value of the changemaker playbook process, then, lies in its ability to help you reframe your thinking, retrain your focus, and prioritize what's solvable. Whether it leads to implementing a new tool or creating a new technical solution or business model, the process strengthens your ability to think deeply and completely without getting off track.

Are there stumbling blocks to using this process effectively? Yes, the ability to be a flexible thinker is chief among them and reinforces my earlier assertion regarding the myth of perfection: Even the most well-defined process cannot identify every issue, or lead you to an effective solution every time. On this, it's key that you remember a basic truth and rule of thumb in changemaking—pursue an 80 percent confidence level. This is true for many reasons, and highlights the importance of flexible thinking: Getting increasingly close to a successful path relies on an ability to observe the effects of the steps you take and your ability to continually adjust your plan based on what you learn. As you develop a habit of observing and refining your plan, you'll also discover that it has a way of breeding greater and greater self-confidence, which in turn creates new openings to solve far more than you ever imagined.

You will continually observe throughout the book that the right process provides both the freedom to think more creatively and the guardrails to help you from becoming overwhelmed by the possibilities. This becomes more and more important to your success when using the playbook, because only after you overcome the perception that a problem must be fully and completely understood can you then hone your natural abilities to spot the opportunities to create change, and move on to the true hardest part of achieving it: plunging into action itself.

I call it the *doing.* You'll soon realize that your ability to *execute* on an action plan is what ultimately separates those who succeed in creating new futures from those who don't. And that the tireless commitment to the refinement cycle, continually refining your actions—correcting and adjusting your plan as the circumstances require—is key to your success.

To further prepare yourself, it's time to revisit the customer service example once again, and learn the other steps of this process. Some version of them will be needed before you are ready to make the full shift from settling on the goals you pursue, to creating the action plan with the greatest potential to achieve them. Continuing with the service example, once we had a sufficient understanding of the issues negatively impacting the customer experience and identified what must change, we shifted our focus to exploring *how.*

The following process steps consistently applied to many situations aimed to improve business operational issues and are key to the *refinement cycle* you will add to your playbook:

1. First, we *redefined the steps. Both manual and automated* were needed to achieve a consistent service—the same or comparable capabilities regardless of why, how, and when customers access it.
2. We *then assessed the new technological capabilities and tools* that could be used to ensure that new steps are both feasible and achievable.
3. We also identified or redefined *roles* that may be needed for each person bearing some responsibility in the success of steps 1 and 2.
4. We zeroed in on any activities that could be replaced, improved, or perhaps eliminated as a result, and the actions required to do so.

Figures 3.1–3.5 are real examples of this process in action. They illustrate the result of a gap analysis that emerged, how it led to an overall theme for the actions we identified, and how to think through the various alternatives in order to refine your plan of action.

Remember, while making informed moves that turn your desired changes from ideas into concrete actions is your North Star, your initial judgment will never be completely accurate. However, you need to reflect upon difficulties that might arise along the way so that in addition to being a flexible plan, it will also be one that's fortified against the challenges and issues that are most likely to block your progress.

Above all, *act*: Move with purpose, determination, and persistence to execute your plan.

A final key takeaway from this chapter dedicated to process is that when it comes to being a changemaker, it's wise for you to assume that you are playing a *long game.*

long game, n.: An approach that requires patience and foresight, with the knowledge that a series of smaller, short-term goals must be met before the larger, long-term one can be achieved.

Recognize that successfully addressing a problem with any degree of complexity requires that you stay the course, experiment with the solutions you choose, and *sometimes that you go back to the drawing board altogether.*

You will find that quick fixes are mostly myth and not appropriate for engaging in meaningful efforts that can achieve the real, lasting impact you're trying to effect. If you dive into your effort to manifest change with this in mind and integrate it into this process all along the way, it will make following it much easier on the whole, and—believe it or not—even fun!

Gaps between operational infrastructure and strategic goals established

Identified Gaps
- Call center technology does not allow for full integration of phone and web-based response to customer inquiries.
- Customer surveys reveal inconsistent practices when interacting with the branch, phone, and internet to fulfill sales needs leading to higher abandonment rates. Branch and customer service center agents have access to different customer information.
- Some customer service phone calls go to branch staff (as opposed to the direct customer service center), leaving branch staff with less time to sell. Individual branch phone numbers are currently listed on the website.

Hypotheses
- Customer confusion is caused by inconsistent sales and service practices across different delivery channels.
- Branch staff's ability to maximize sales efforts is hampered by routine customer service inquiries.

Emerging redesign theme
- Upgrade call center technology to more efficiently handle customer inquiries through multiple communication channels and focus branch platform staff on sales challenges by removing call volume and providing improved customer information.

Figure 3.1   Gap analysis leads to future state theme development.

Source: Branch network/direct distribution channels

Themes and ideas developed

Approved theme
Create consistent sales and service processes for all delivery channels by providing common customer information for branch and customer service center agents, rerouting inquiries to an enhanced VRU, and integrating voice/web-based sales and service delivery.

Ideas
- Consider innovative multimedia contact center solutions that include web-based solutions such as text chat and email response in addition to the traditional IVR.
- Provide branch and multimedia contact center agents with online access to common customer information to maximize sales and service effectiveness and ensure a positive customer experience.
- Consolidate rerouting of calls and migrate customers to web-based response units at the customer's preference.

Benefits
- Increase customer satisfaction by handling sales and service, reducing wait time, and increasing customer and staff satisfaction.
- Enable branch staff to focus on in-person sales and service.

Figure 3.1   *Continued*

Customer needs	Process stumbling blocks	Possible emerging redesign theme
• Customer-focused, consistent marketing and sales approach. • Access to specialized investment products and tailored advice for successful financial planning (including investment strategy, tax strategy, and trust and estate planning). • Integrated marketing and sales platform providing customers with information on an array of investment products and options as well as complementary banking services. • Dedicated personal financial planner in the branch network or full capacity delivery channels such as telebanking and internet that offer investment management and research around the clock.	• **Redundant product offerings across multiple investment management subsidiaries.** • **Sales and marketing efforts are being duplicated across the organization.** • **Customer confusion on what, how, and who to call to purchase investment products.** • **Call center has limited knowledge or access to information on investment products and services.**	• Differentiate sales and service delivery infrastructure for investment services across subsidiaries to reflect client profitability and needs. • Sales effectiveness through an integrated investment sales force offering a consistent product set across all delivery channels. • In essence become the one-stop full-service financial center that can provide customer's every investment and banking need. • Utilize call center for inbound customer servicing as well as outbound telemarketing efforts. Train customer service representatives to exploit cross-selling opportunities for basic investment products. • Leverage data warehouse to eliminate duplicate marketing efforts and identify cross-selling opportunities.

Figure 3.2   Developing themes for future state customer experience redesign. Linking themes to already defined corporate strategies and aligning them with the strategic objectives of each line of business.

1. Understand current infrastructure, process, and strategy for retention measurement and tracking, cross sales, customer servicing, and customer information management.

2. Evaluate root cause of customer dissatisfaction from exit surveys and historical customer information.

3. Work in conjunction with marketing to analyze MCIF system, or similar database, at the household level (e.g., top decile profitability analysis/product mix) or account level, if possible.

4. Identify current product offering (including strength and weakness analysis) with product management and also provide best-of-breed products in market.

5. Evaluate current problem resolution protocol from identification to resolution response.

6. Perform rigorous assumption testing of recommended in overall design (with DCT, marketing, legal, etc.).

7. Refine model with strategic input from top management.

8. Outline detailed implementation plan.

Figure 3.3   Theme validation—customer satisfaction and loyalty.

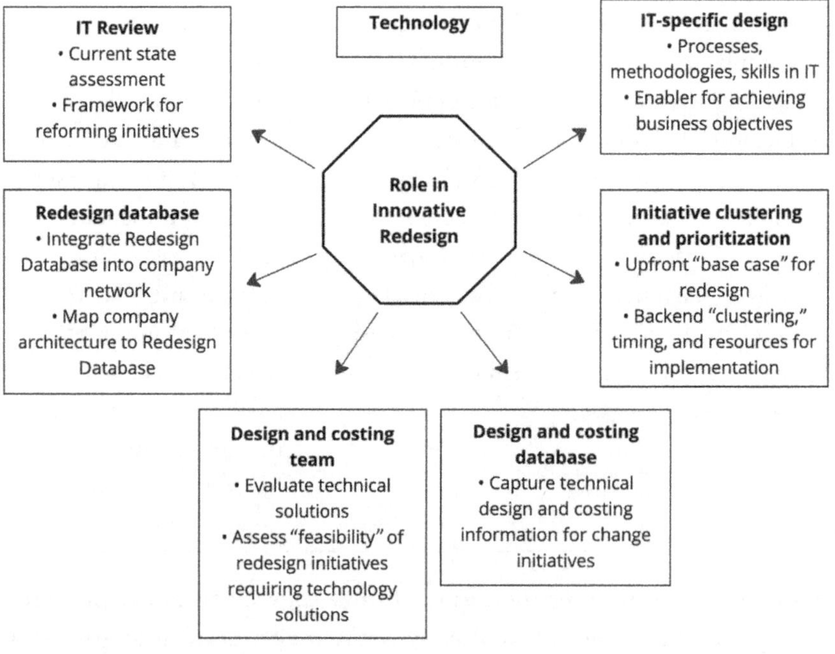

Figure 3.4   Role of technology.

1. Is it a modular and scalable system?
2. Does it support intelligent routing?
3. Can it be deployed rapidly?
4. Does it support network routing?
5. Can it be easily integrated in other front and back office applications?
6. Does it support multiple contact media: telephone, email, web?
7. Does it effectively manage the contact queue to meet service-level agreements?
8. Does it provide management tools to ensure effectiveness and efficiency?
9. Does it allow blending of customer service representatives among inbound and outbound tasks and telephone and online contact media?

Source: Strategy Partners International, Choosing the Right Customer Contact Solution, May 2000.

Figure 3.5   Theme refinement—future state customer experience.

Key Takeaways

The goal of this chapter was to explain the process methodology that is utilized across the various scenarios shared in this book. It explains the power of the *changemaker playbook process* and its importance to the success you have in your efforts to achieve real impact. It helps you see that the ability to contribute to change doesn't require genius—at least not in the traditional sense—but rather that you maintain a certain discipline in the way you think about solving a problem and how you prepare to tackle change. This, in turn, will feed your confidence for plunging fully into the challenge at hand. You may note that the progress you make does not completely eliminate the issue, but doesn't have to because the meaningful impact it does have will bring you that much closer to achieving your goals. Most importantly, the process empowers you to make an all-important shift in your perception

(continued)

(continued)

of the difficulty involved. You've learned the difference between the current and future state, where the disconnects are, and *why*. More than anything, though, mastering your use of this process helps you understand your individual potential to affect some of the world's most difficult problems.

Here's a review of the changemaker playbook process elements for your quick reference:

1. Inform your perspective by considering both the current versus future state of the issue at hand.
2. Perform a gap analysis. Assess differences between how things are currently done/occurring and how they would ideally work.
3. Brainstorm ideas that answer the question "What's the fix?" Identify ways to augment or replace parts of the current workflows by adding a new tool, role, or some other practical solution.
4. Set a plan. Decide on the actions you will implement in order to proceed based on the priority/best potential.
5. Take action.
6. Observe, learn, refine, and repeat.

But I am not quite finished on this topic. In Chapter 4, you learn more about mastering the changemaker playbook process by learning about the art of the pivot.

4

Process Part II: The Art of the Pivot

Remember, your ability to execute well is the key to effecting any change at all. As you've seen, this in turn requires that you maintain a steadfast commitment to the process I shared in the last chapter and staying clear that any problem worth solving requires a measured yet flexible and forward-thinking approach. There are many reasons these principles hold true that you'll continue to observe throughout the examples I provide in the coming chapters.

As you do, take note of the way each example I share reinforces how the changemaker playbook process specifically helps you structure your thinking, stay on track, and get into position to take action. You'll also learn how the need to stay flexible comes into play, and ways to adjust along the way, both of which sit at the very heart of your success. Sometimes, depending on the situation you encounter, you may even decide through the process to replace your original plan altogether! If this happens, there is no need to panic; in fact, it may mean you can have even more impact than you first assumed. That's why this chapter is dedicated to sharing another crucial piece of the playbook with you: *the art of the pivot.*

I'll first set the stage. Over 20 years ago, the internet, as in most areas of business and our life, was the start of a total transformation in our use of media. As a result, it profoundly changed media as an industry as well.

Digital media became a completely new way to connect with consumers, and to sell products and services to them. This also became a critical juncture in my work, at the time as an advisor to businesses looking to accelerate the achievement of their strategic goals—and thus in my changemaking journey. It proved a vital opportunity for me to apply and refine my own approach to changemaking. I'll explore how this is relevant to you as an aspiring changemaker, in this chapter.

Problem-Solving in a Sea of Uncertainty: The BrightLine Pivot

With the explosion of the internet, Google dominated as the online platform and shaped our experience. Soon after, it set off a proliferation of new marketing techniques for brands selling us all our favorite products. This early experience with the internet was not ideal—it was a frustrating and chaotic environment, where you might see ads (called popups) that distracted you from your browsing session and became a major annoyance. That said, it did provide an opportunity for the first time since the invention of the telephone to dynamically interact with people. Soon organizations both big and small created websites, and they became ubiquitous as both a source of information and a platform for promoting products. Soon after that, interactive video was born and began to replace the static digital "billboard"—from there, everything we assumed about ways to use video changed forever.

Now let's take a brief step back to introduce a few new terms:

digital media, n.: Digitized information displayed or broadcasted through a screen, including text, audio, video, and image.

interactive experience, n.: A two-way encounter whereby the viewer is actively involved in what they are shown.

Social media followed the earliest forms of digital media. The main point here is that with all these new changes to the media experience, our expectations as consumers and users of these online communication vehicles began to shift as well, to a more two-way, interactive dynamic.

Before that, television was by far the single most prevalent and important medium for communication, whether for news, sports, movies, or other programming consumed in this way. Other than movie theaters, television defined the collective experience with video content. Every bit of this content other than what we watched on the public broadcast channel was paid for by the brands that sponsored it, and in return they received mentions and what the marketplace came to know as the 30-second spot.

30-second spot, n.: A 30-second TV commercial.

It was obvious that TV as a medium would ultimately collide with the internet. There was virtually no one who didn't see the convergence of the two as inevitable, although there were many ways to guess how it would actually happen—what would tip it off, as they say. But when it did, how the television could be used as a form of communication would clearly have to change too. Within this context, my co-founders and I created BrightLine, a company developed with a value proposition to bring these fundamentally new consumer experiences on the internet to the television medium. The idea was that major consumer brands would also need to ready themselves for the inevitable changes that the internet would foist upon their TV communication strategy.

So, just like the approach I took to bring the current state more in line with where the future seemed to be headed in the banking examples shared, I used a clean sheet of paper to sketch out what we could imagine about the future state for television. In this case, that translated into thinking about how the medium would be forced to change once the internet collided with it. We created a very specific value proposition for our business that reflected our vision of a transformed TV medium that combined the best parts of the television experience with the best new capabilities that the internet offered—the potential for turning the TV viewer experience into a way for viewers to have a dialogue with their favorite brands.

The vision led to a business model (see Figure 4.1) that made it possible for brands who relied most on the TV medium to communicate the relative value of their products to consumers, and our company BrightLine was launched to support them in that process—specifically, to guide them on ways to revise their TV advertising strategy to both account for and feed these new behaviors.

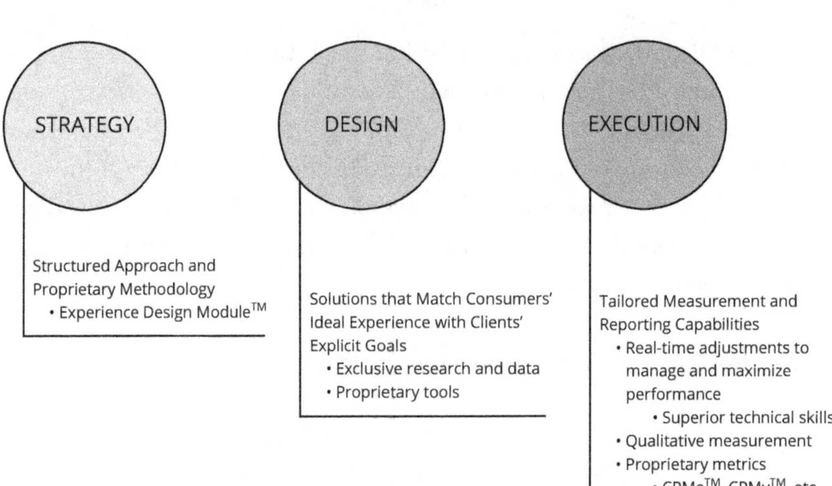

Figure 4.1   BrightLine's essential role in TV's changing world.

We created a turnkey solution (see Figure 4.2) for them to reshape their use of
TV in this manner, and gain firsthand insight on how to do so in the most effective ways. BrightLine provided a process and unique set of skills to accomplish
our clients' particular goals, and a self-reinforcing way for them to constantly
learn from the viewers' response to these methods, over and over again.

First:	Next:	After 6 months:
• Take specific steps to identify the ideal experience for target consumers (Experience Design Module™) • Establish the most meaningful measures for determining the power of TV as a medium to reach the new consumer • Develop sample ad experiences that achieve a desired look, feel, function • Identify solutions that achieve the desired experience and meet requirements for measuring impact	• Refine attributes, ideal experience profile as necessary • Identify specific goals for planned marketing initiatives • Evaluate upcoming creative and marketing initiatives against preliminary TV feature opportunity continuum	• Balance internal and external requirements of messaging and media outlets • Foster dialogue/interplay during key planning stages for seamless integration • Require coordination among media, creative, and interactive teams to develop fully integrated campaign proposals

Repeat on a regular and systematic basis

Figure 4.2   The process.

Notice how the language BrightLine used with the company's clients matches the terms introduced to you in past chapters to build your own playbook. BrightLine represents another example of the changemaker process in action you've observed thus far—as illustrated in Figures 4.3 and 4.4, the "ideal consumer experience" seen in the banking example, became the "ideal viewer experience," In addition, the method used to show the way to move from the current state to the future state in the banking case is not dissimilar to the one used to help BrightLine's brand clients move from the current state to the future state of TV's role in their ad strategy.

The process approach used to help clients navigate from the current to the future state in television at this time came purely from applying a templated approach, called the *Experience Design Module* (EDM), which gave companies a straightforward way to think about the vast potential that the internet might represent to amplify the value of their products to TV viewers (see Figures 4.5 and 4.6). This was true because in the earliest stages of the transformation that finally occurred, there were only limited opportunities for brands to learn in this way. In fact, there were many attempts to make TV an interactive medium since the very birth of the television—the remote control itself can be counted as one of the first to really catch on. That said, a few stand out as part of this story as more groundbreaking in light of how we view interactivity today.

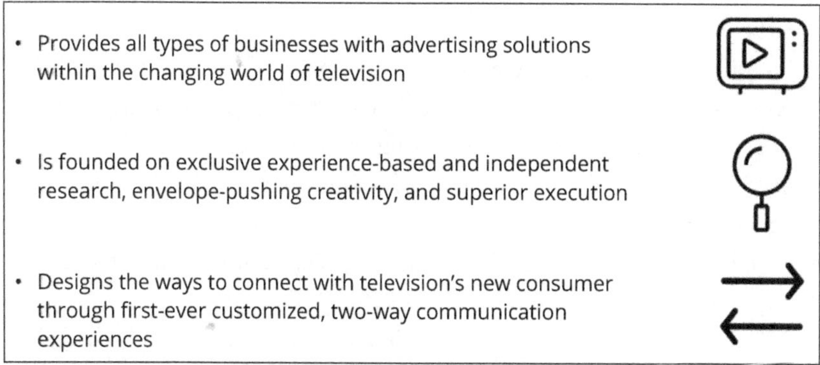

Figure 4.3 BrightLine's ideal viewer experience model.

It begins with knowing all the possible ways to use advanced features function.

Requirements for staying relevant amid substantial and dynamic shifts in viewer behavior:

1. **A vision** for consumers' ideal experience with a brand, product, and messaging
2. Continuously **aggregating and distilling** the array of TV's new functions to fit the vision
3. **Designing ad experiences** that capitalize on BrightLine's singular deep innovations in the space
4. **Flexibly managing execution** with real-time adjustments that deliver on the commitment

Figure 4.4   Captivating viewers is the road to staying relevant with TV audiences.

Are customers willing to engage with content from brands and what are the dynamics of that engagement?

- Assess viewers' inclination to opt-in to a branded interactive television experience.
- Identify features viewers will be most interested in using/experiencing.
- Assess viewers' willingness to repeatedly return to a brand experience.
- Locate the sweet spot for maximizing viewer duration.
- Understand how content influences viewer behavior and campaign performance.
- Design promotion points that are most effective at driving viewer engagement.
- Assess relative impact of interactive TV on advertising brand recall, intent to buy, etc.
- Understand viewer response to targeted messaging by geographic location or demographic profile.

Figure 4.5   Understanding the customer's expectations.

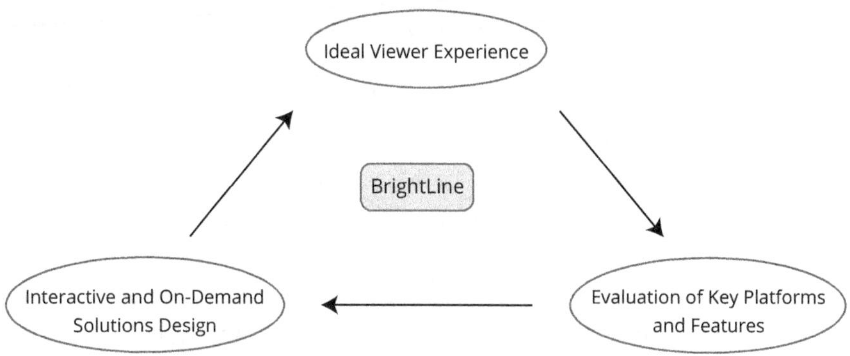

Figure 4.6   BrightLine's ideal viewer experience flow.

TiVo is a very clear example. First introduced in 1999, TiVo (along with satellite TV providers like DIRECTV and the Dish Network, though secondarily so) is broadly credited for a breakthrough in remote control interactivity and television viewing. This also marked the first time that the digital video recorder (DVR) became widely available, which allowed viewers to record, pause, and rewind live television—and this fundamentally changed how TV audiences interacted with video content. This innovation gave viewers unprecedented control over what they watched and when they watched it, freeing them from the constraints of broadcast schedules and enabling features like "binge-watching" long before the streaming services we may associate with that term became mainstream.

binge-watching, v.: Continuous watching of a TV show or other form of visual content for a long time without stopping.

This level of interactivity that allowed viewers to navigate complex menus, schedule recordings, and receive tailored recommendations—all using the remote control—was a significant historic leap over traditional TV remotes, which were limited to basic channel and volume controls. However, even at the height of its popularity, TiVo never achieved wide enough adoption to replace the way most people watched TV. This would come almost 20 years later.

It's important to understand that the value of the Experience Design Module to BrightLine's clients was not its ability to bring the broad interactive capabilities of the internet to TV on behalf of the brands who used it, but rather to give them the opportunity to learn how they would take full advantage of these capabilities as the TV and internet continued to merge. It was simply not possible when BrightLine was first launched to know the timeframe, let alone the technologies, that would dominate once the medium finished its transformation, but our bet was that those who already understood how to reach and connect with their consumers through a two-way interaction would most definitely have an edge against those who did not.

The Experience Design Module was a templated approach for its time with all the hallmarks of your playbook—a flexible model that allowed BrightLine's clients to continuously reshape the ways they chose to create a two-way experience with the unique capabilities of each distinct TV platform. Constant adjustments were made to incorporate new insights on the most effective types of experiences as they were generated, and allowed for a continuous loop of refinement in strategy.

Then everything changed. In 2016 the convergence we long predicted would inevitably occur began to take hold and accelerate, taking the form of what you now know as TV streaming. Streaming became the route by which the internet would transform the TV experience forever.

streaming, n.: A way to watch shows, movies, or live channels over the internet without needing cable or satellite.

The Pivot

You now have the full backdrop for learning the crucial lesson of this chapter: the ability to pivot. The most important thing to take away from BrightLine's story so far is that the approach and model that served the market so well as the future state unfolded to become a reality no one could predict ultimately needed to be remade in its entirety. As the long-anticipated convergence of the two mediums actually took place, BrightLine's approach to providing its unique value had to change entirely to reflect this brand-new form of television. BrightLine's wherewithal to guide brands on the changing viewer behavior that streaming unleashed had to change right along with it.

It was no longer enough to continue adding the original value the company became known for—a new version had to be created, from scratch. It wasn't sufficient for Version 2 to rely on refinements to an existing methodology as it had up to that point, either; this time would involve a redo that replaced the process template with a solution that changed the role technology played in BrightLine's business proposition fundamentally and permanently, as well. The EDM was replaced with a proprietary software that built upon the extensive insight BrightLine collected over time, that's capable of actually creating the ideal viewer experience. Moreover, the solution has been built to automatically build and deliver the experiences it creates, too, across every individual platform that provides viewers with a way to stream their favorite programming on their TV.

Advancements in internet-connected set-tops and smart TVs have allowed for unprecedented leaps in audience engagement potential and have since generated an expansive crop of streaming TV video offerings. What makes BrightLine's technology solution so powerful in this changed world is that each new capability introduced brings a host of new and unique and new complexities with it—most notably a highly fragmented web of disparate computer code bases, video delivery paths, and operating systems needed in order to maximize their potential and use. This is where BrightLine's technology software shines; it has the ability to bridge the differences across all these streaming devices and apps, allowing for an ad experience to be designed and delivered seamlessly across them all. To provide the solution, an automated design studio was built allowing brands to create their own two-way viewer experience, as well as a software development kit (SDK) that takes the uniqueness of each TV platform out of the equation, and a data management platform to support the brand's ability to learn from the decisions they make and adjust accordingly. As a result, they achieve their own ideal viewer experiences and provide them at maximum scale across each and every streaming provider and internet-enabled device, all without any concern for the technical nuances of the TV streaming ecosystem.

operating system, n.: The software inside a TV connected to the internet that lets you use apps, stream shows, and control the TV. It manages how you interact with the TV and what features or streaming services you can access.

> *software development kit* (SDK), n.: A set of tools and resources that help developers build apps for internet-enabled TVs or streaming devices without starting from scratch.

BrightLine's shift in business models worked because the pivot we made to replace the process template with a technology solution was timely, years of insight could be draw upon to help our clients take full advantage of TV's digital transformation, and thanks to the company's incredibly committed management, investors, and clients, we were able to successfully play the *long game*. When TV's evolution to a true digital experience came, the complexities of using it as a medium for true two-way interactivity was a veritable nightmare, and BrightLine's technology became once again a solution for its time.

There is much more to the company story that may interest and perhaps even inspire some changemakers, but that's a topic for a different playbook. The point I am focused on here is that the process you are becoming increasingly familiar with served as the structured yet flexible path by which two very different business propositions were created to address the same fundamental need. Each had its own value and proven ability to drive impact; each reflected a route for bridging the current state with the future state, even when so many of their characteristics were not possible to know; and each achieved a market-leading position in the television industry.

BrightLine's story speaks to one of the basic truths encountered time and time again when taking action with impact—your level of success as a changemaker is very often determined by your ability to adapt to shifting circumstances, and your best chances of spotting the moments for doing so will come from your relentless effort toward continuous refinement. This is the basis for mastering the art of the pivot. In BrightLine's case, the challenge that the internet represented for how to best use TV as a communication vehicle remained the same—how to best reach the consumer—but as the television medium morphed, so too did the company's first business model have to be replaced. Indeed, the entire basis of our proposition had fallen out of step with how TV was changing, and forced us to go back to the drawing board completely. In the end, the changemaker playbook process, and our commitment to the refinement cycle, allowed the company to pivot and fulfill its original vision: Provide a solution that achieves a viewer experience in line with the new behaviors that the onset of the internet set in motion more than a decade before.

Key Takeaways

Placing the changemaker playbook process at the heart of your efforts as a changemaker provides you with a proven, reliable approach for understanding the lengths of your personal abilities and potential to create change with impact.

You must now add another key aspect to your playbook—the ability to take action at the breakneck speed that will be required to meaningfully improve upon the rate of progress needed to contribute to the world's most vexing issues. Get ready to dig in to understand why and how your awareness of the most modern and advanced technologies become a crucial factor, and how to apply them to reach mission-critical milestones at top speed.

Transforming with Tech

In this part, the book's emphasis shifts to train your sights on the dramatic effects of utilizing the most modern tools available in support of the playbook. It illustrates how advanced technologies support and enable the disciplined, structured, and flexible thinking embedded in the playbook, allowing you to capture a whole new level of possibility.

This part walks through the particular and vital role that digital technology and AI play when taking actions of consequence. Examples are used to illustrate how this is so, from the most basic to the transformational.

- Chapter 5 describes the capabilities of the most sophisticated technologies available and illustrates what they can yield when they are at the center of a clean sheet of paper design.
- Chapter 6 builds on the examples provided in Chapter 5 to look at the unprecedented role that AI plays. It also explains the confidence that can be derived in relieving the pressure you may feel to be an expert in all aspects of the situation at hand.

5

Tech for Good: A Tool and Path to Transformation

This chapter switches gears from establishing the process at the center of your playbook to illustrate how to identify the action paths with the greatest potential for driving impact. While process is key to what you achieve, it's still just that: a process. Ensuring that your actions can lead to the most meaningful outcomes, however, is achieved by utilizing the most modern *tools* available. Combining what the changemaker playbook process can achieve with the right tools will always help ensure that you are in the strongest possible position to succeed with the highest levels of efficiency and effectiveness.

Like the previous chapters, context is important for exploring these principles more easily. Translating your ideas into action is challenging, logically and for all the reasons I've reviewed with you thus far. As my illustrations show, even the best-laid plans require regular adjustments to correct, tweak, and even eliminate certain elements in order to clear the inevitable roadblocks that pop up along the way. Previous examples illustrated how issues are broken down as they emerge using the steps of your changemaker playbook process to navigate them. But as you are hopefully beginning to also see, you're not just using the guidelines in these pages to build a static playbook, but a flexible, resilient, *modern* one. And as you'll now see, utilizing the most advanced technologies available as well as the strongest capabilities possible takes on a special significance in this regard.

I begin simply, because you'll often find that technology is just a means to an end—a relatively simple tool that helps you implement your plan— but technology can just as often turn out to be the solution itself, as you saw with the BrightLine example I shared in the last chapter. This is an important distinction to make when implementing an action plan that I will cover in greater depth in the next chapter. In this one I will be covering the former—technology as a tool for achieving efficiencies.

As touched on previously, many of the business situations I've personally managed simultaneously involved many products, services, and operational functions. Figure 5.1 gives you an example of this. More often than not, there were numerous overlaps across these areas as well, and in these situations, technology proved an integral tool for addressing them. We also found that we could overcome much of the inherent complexity of these situations by looking at products and businesses not just in isolation, but at their linkages—that is, from end to end. When doing so, we discovered that the overlaps and linkages could always be better understood by using technology as a tool. Most often, we used specially designed databases and process facilitation software to accomplish this, and both ended up becoming the key to getting to the root of issues and identifying appropriate solutions.

On this basis, I make what may seem a bold claim to you: Technology plays a particular and indispensable role in your ability to take consequential action.

consequential action, n.: An action that creates tangible, measurable results.

To get a closer look at this role I revisit the customer service situation once again. Although it's not the most profound example, it will help you continue building your basic understanding of this aspect of changemaking before moving on to the larger, more broad-based solutions you can pursue—the ones with global impact, among others.

Redesign team	Process groups
Investments	• Investments under advice • Investments under administration • Investments under management
Branch division	• Metropolitan branch network • State and territory branch network
Electronic/direct	• Operations • Direct banking • Electronic banking
Mortgage/ consumer lending	• Network mortgage lending • Personal consumer lending • Third-party mortgage origination • Mortgage operations/securities • Consumer and commercial collections/ recovery
Commercial	• Treasury • Risk management • Automotive finance • Business banking • Corporate banking
Information technology	• IT development • IT production
Support services	• Facilities • Finance • HR • Marketing/communications
Cross corporate	• Purchasing • Policy

Figure 5.1 Future state redesign components.

Utilizing Tech to Solve Complex Problems

In the previous chapter I explained that products and services must often be supported by a number of technical systems. You could see through the examples that these can differ from one another substantially, and when they do, how the customer experiences across them also differ as a result. In one example, a customer requested help through a virtual assistant with the capability to respond quickly and accurately by querying a database or using AI-generated responses. As you saw, instant access to the right data enabled a rapid and helpful response. In contrast, many live representatives do not have instant access to the same or even similar customer data, and are therefore unable to provide the same level or quality of service.

In cases like these, the most effective and reliable way to align the two is to replace the systems that the live representative can access with the latest technical hardware and software solutions available. As illustrated, it allows them to fully address major inconsistencies in service quality, bring them into better sync, and provide a common and more seamless interaction.

This path of action may sound like a simple fix, and fairly straightforward, but the reality was just the opposite. To affect the technical and process changes that were needed, whole data systems had to be integrated; technical interfaces across customer contact points had to be developed, algorithms needed to be written, and next-level automation capabilities had to be put in place in order to achieve these improvements in service quality, accuracy, and response time.

You might think "businesses have been using technology to increase efficiency and reduce cost forever—this is hardly novel." And that's of course true—using technology in situations like these does seem a fairly obvious solution. But the point isn't to "wow" you with the revelation that computers are a revolutionary way to help your business—it's to make a broader point. The example demonstrates how technology becomes instrumental to taking consequential action in ways no other field of knowledge is doing. In its ability to contribute to improving if not totally solving almost any problem, technology is truly in a league of its own.

When viewed through this lens, the data systems, technical interfaces, and automation capabilities that were implemented in the service example were no less critical to solving the problems affecting the customer than rocket science was to solving the problems faced by Apollo 13. In both situations, technology was a means for building or otherwise creating new capabilities that directly impacted those affected, and few would disagree that this is crucial for any business. It also shows that technology is increasingly a constant for effecting needed change at the micro level, and transformational change at the micro as well as macro level. As such, it is also a vital component in your personal changemaker's playbook.

Given its particular role in raising the level and quality of a customer's experience, technology is invaluable in companies both big and small. But its capacity is even more exciting to observe in the next example I'll share. It's an exemplary illustration that shows how technology can become the path that can fundamentally redefine a company's actual *identity*!

One of the most exciting business change situations I've had a rare opportunity to experience personally involved the complete and total change of a company's entire business model and strategy. It puts an even finer point on why I've dedicated this part of the book to technology's versatility and essential place in your playbook. It's also a crisp and exciting example of consequential action.

The story begins with a bank called Signet, known at that time for its commitment to providing customers exceptional service and innovative products designed just for them. The company took six months to carry out a change program across the entire corporation that followed the changemaker playbook process established in Part II. However, unlike the other examples I've shared, Signet decided to go much further than using the latest software and hardware solutions to bring different customer touchpoints—branches, call centers, and ATMs—into alignment. Instead, they decided to rebuild every single one of their businesses, products, and services around *one* leading-edge customer technology platform. The enormity of this undertaking cannot be overstated; it meant deconstructing each and every one of the individual processes that supported each of these areas, redefining every staff role, and totally replacing all of the supporting systems their business depended on at the time. In essence, they were starting from square one.

To put this in its fullest context, Signet's future state meant turning its mostly manual and tangled mass of activities and workflows upside down and inside out—replacing all with a first-of-its-kind platform that completely revolved around the customer experience. In other words, they applied the approach applied in previous examples in the context of one area of the company's business across their entire corporation. None of this would have been possible without using all the cutting-edge capabilities that technology afforded them. It was a groundbreaking and truly inspiring show of leadership and commitment to customer impact and transformational change.

In the next section I'll take the topic of consequential action to a completely different realm. It touches on business considerations, but perhaps you'll find it an even more exciting example of how to raise your personal impact potential to a world level.

Creating SustainChain

You first learned the foundational step of building your playbook in Chapter 2—break down complex situations by asking basic questions. Each of the examples shared since have presented different cases on how to take that step. At a very high level we also took a basic stab early on at deconstructing world-scale problems—specifically climate risks, health, food, and water security. I pick up that thread now to show how to put the changemaker process into action on these huge issues, pulling from my personal experiences in economic change and development. Note that, in the examples that follow, I am about to share how the immense and complex nature of climate change becomes a near-perfect lens for reflecting on the value of the changemaker playbook process, and the playbook itself. Hopefully it will also be both a source of additional inspiration and boost your confidence that bold action with impact is within your grasp, even on enormous problems.

In 2019, I began puzzling through the challenges that organizations of different sizes and kinds, profit and nonprofit alike, were experiencing in their efforts to move their sustainability and climate change programs forward. It started, as always, by trying to get to the bottom of what was primarily blocking them from making meaningful and sustainable progress.

I began in a way that should now be familiar to you—that is, by reflecting on what achieving sustainability would actually mean in the most practical terms possible.

sustainability, n.: The capacity to fulfill present needs in a lasting way, that also safeguards the environment and ensuring the well-being of future generations.

I tried first to envision the future state—in this case the actual *future*—a world that had achieved sustainability. In order not to become totally over-whelmed by what seemed a countless number of issues and factors that would no doubt lie beneath, I started by reflecting on the more obvious and most fundamental things a sustainable future would need to ensure without causing further damage to our planet—concluding that they are secure access to sustainable sources of food, water, and energy. After all, I thought, the chances of humanity's survival without these are (to use a phrase from the Apollo 13 example) slim to none. After training my focus on these three objectives, I probed deeper to home in on the biggest factors driving our human potential to positively affect these challenges and to break them down.

Shortly thereafter, the COVID-19 health pandemic hit hard across the globe, and laid bare just how critical well-functioning supply chains are to sustaining human life. In that moment, we collectively experienced the ways that a serious disruption to global supply chains was able to stop the flow of products we relied on and shut down whole markets. In that critical moment, we also collectively realized that the world economy's ability to fully function hinges on having robust supply chains in place and flowing without serious blockage. That shared experience highlighted a basic truth: Addressing the worsening effects of weather-related events on food, water, and energy will require resilient global supply chains that are built to with-stand the impact of extreme climate conditions.

resilience, n.: The ability to adapt, recover, and thrive amid challenges, disturbances, or adversity, maintaining essential functions and well-being.

Luckily, as you'll see in coming examples, building resilience into sup-ply chains is a topic we can collectively agree on, despite the polarized views on climate change overall. Indeed, as you'll begin to note throughout the book, our ability to maintain healthy supply chains is just one of many pieces of the climate and sustainability puzzle that we can all agree is impor-tant, news cycles and political atmosphere notwithstanding.

Continuing with the example, by focusing squarely on the life-sustaining elements of food, water, and energy in the common context of our human experience with the pandemic, I was able to look at the possibilities for change, just as Newton did, from a new and different angle that inspired and provided me with a direction to creatively search for a path to action.

Rebuilding global supply chains across industries and geographies is an extremely tall task. And, understandably, this is usually the point where most people will drop the pencil. But as you'll see, it can also be the very point in the changemaking process where your playbook begins to light the way. Indeed, while supply chains seem a pretty unlikely comparison on the surface—how similar can customer service and global sustainability be?—there is actually a highly similar approach to tackling the array of considerations for moving from the current to future state in both cases.

In this case, of course, there is another dimension that poses an additional and imposing challenge, given the many who seriously question whether the business community has a genuine intention to address the structural deficiencies that block creation of resilient and sustainable supply chains. Given the considerable added time, attention, and effort these changes require, as well as business's primary focus on revenue growth and the bottom line, these are of course fair and important questions. Indeed, insincerity on assurances made can be proven—the issue of *greenwashing* is widely evidenced by data that shows substantial gaps between stated commitments to climate resilience in the private sector and the actions businesses have made to their models and supply chains to achieve needed outcomes.

> *greenwashing*, n.: The act of exaggerating or misrepresenting a company's environmental commitments, creating a gap between what they promise publicly and the real changes they make in their business practices.

While this is important to bear in mind, this book is not the place to debate the will of the business community to invest in building resilient supply chains. That being said, a few practical realities may be positive indicators and worthy of quick mention before I move on:

- First, at the heart of operational efficiency and profitability for a business is the age-old question of "at what cost?" Increasingly, the answer to this question shifts toward the potentially heavy cost to a company's viability over time of not addressing issues of resilience.

- Second, for those who fear that businesses just don't care, there is a vibrant investment community bringing financial support to businesses that do care. It acts as a powerful incentive for companies to drive toward sustainability innovations that help solve these problems.
- Finally, the fact that greenwashing exists may ironically be a good sign. Many, myself included, feel that this would not be so if businesses didn't feel the need to make promises to address these issues in the first place.

These points also serve to reinforce one another and may represent a natural and enormous source of potential and hope.

Regardless, the difficulty of moving from the current state to the future state to achieve resilience in global supply chains is immense and overwhelming. For the reasons reviewed and many more, this is to be expected. However, one of the characteristics this challenge shares with earlier examples is the tremendous amount of overlap among the various hurdles to overcome. In fact, all the major steps involved—from sourcing to manufacturing to product delivery and sales—share many of the same basic requirements in order to get to the future state as other business challenges might. And there's another revelation that technology puts an increasingly fine point and highlights—you actually don't have to be an expert on a particular area that requires change to be an instrumental source of progress and impact. There are, as in each case explored so far, fixes hiding in plain sight, visible to anyone with the drive to dig through and find them, regardless of their area or level of expertise. This will become more apparent as you proceed through the chapter.

For now I will continue with the story. By continuing to apply the playbook's framework, I looked next at ways to identify the most obvious (and difficult) problems to overcome, and set my sights on deciding my focus and identifying my actions by using the current versus future state comparison demonstrated in previous chapters. Looking at sustainability as the future state, I asked, "What must absolutely be in place that isn't currently in order to reach that future?" and the systems we rely on to ensure safe and sustainable water, food, and energy supply quickly came into focus. Finally, I asked, "What would need to happen for that future to become reality?"—and with the moments of the COVID-19 pandemic fresh in my mind, the overarching factor of creating sustainable and resilient global supply chains became very clear.

Take a moment to note as we have with past examples how the process at the core of the playbook once again provided the structure and clarity that allowed me to better define the problems to be solved, and helped things feel less daunting. As you'll soon observe the discipline that this structured approach creates was all-important for identifying the steps that immediately followed—this, as first introduced in Chapter 3, is rooted in the ability to shift your attention from *what* is needed to achieve the future state, to *how* to make it real. First, have a look at how the ability to think more clearly translated into a set of concrete and organized actions.

One of the patterns you observed in previous examples is present in this one, as well: There are not only major overlaps in what is needed to rebuild global supply chains, but also similar if not common implementation needs among them—including expertise, money, scientific research, tools, and more. This is where a new and different type of solution that's critical to impacting a problem comes into view, one created *for* the experts instead of *by* them. Indeed, one that requires relatively little specific expertise of a particular industry or even supply chain management at all.

One of the simplest and most encouraging facts about climate change is that there is no shortage of people trying to manage the problem. Indeed, the number of real solutions being attempted and actions being taken—by both experts and others determined to solve these issues—turns out not to be the main issue at all. In addition, a deeper look at the current state reveals that an inordinate number of promising actions are taking place, too copious to even fully account for here. Instead, the biggest stumbling block, aside from the pure volume of activity, is that all of the good work and related actions being taken are extremely fragmented, disconnected, and disorganized. What's more, because of the nature of the actions being taken, many doing good work are often stymied by their lack of access to the right resources, proper funding, needed collaboration, and critical partnerships that would make their contributions available, widely accessible, and used in all the areas that they apply—in other words, scalable.

Rapidly evolving technologies can help solve these intense challenges in fresh ways. They represent the *how* for solving some of the underlying issues that otherwise block progress toward reaching the future state—put in terms first established in the earliest pages of this book, technologies—or rather their unique applications—are part of a fix that hides in plain sight, which doesn't necessarily require supply chain management expertise to uncover, just your changemaker's playbook and a will to help change things for the better.

In my own case, my thoughts and observations on the supply chain issue led me to take out a clean sheet of paper and sketch a technology solution that could help businesses and organizations of all sizes and kinds navigate the morass of actions already taking place to fortify supply chains, and to jump the steep learning curve on where to find the right resources, funding, and other critical partnerships needed to make more, better and faster progress.

How did I do that? What were the considerations? Finally, how can we prescribe a solution given the disparate, fragmented actions taking place, across the universe of actors needed to build supply chains—which involves organizations of all different kinds, people of all different roles, and different types of actions? You will understand these better by observing the following:

Using widely available digital technologies and a particular type of machine learning called reinforcement learning (RL), which I discuss in greater depth in a subsequent chapter and appendix. I was able to sketch out a new platform, which we aptly named SustainChain, where the work of this global community of actors would be visible to one another, and make new and different collaborations possible.

> *reinforcement learning* (RL), n.: A way for computers to learn by trying things out and seeing what works. The more it practices, the better it is at choosing the actions that lead to the best results. By learning this way, the computer can figure out brand new ways to solve problems—even ones it's never seen before. It can "discover" new paths or strategies to reach its goals, and even adapt if things change.

The plan was to use a form of data intelligence that would learn from the actions of every user and instantly convert that learning into relevant suggested actions to other community members. Going even further, by giving this visibility, opportunity for collaboration, and ability to guide users, we could support the work occurring in different areas of focus, like water security and agriculture, across geographies and industries simultaneously. Rebuilding global supply chains, of course, will take all of these things!

The machine learning component became a central part of the design that I'll speak in depth about in the next chapter. In brief, we created an ability within SustainChain to learn from the community and to deliver actionable insights to other members. In this sense, it would do double duty as both an efficiency tool and a guidance system. This would allow those touching a particular part of the supply chain—whether for sourcing raw materials, transportation, manufacturing methods, or distribution systems—to work on filling needs they have in common, together. By giving everyone in the community live access to the information that the AI was generating, new actionable opportunities could constantly be revealed, encouraging members to connect, collaborate, and partner on their common "links" in the chain. If we could build it, I thought, it would provide a real-time ability to connect the dots and to help solve potentially massive challenges.

What makes the idea of a SustainChain hopeful and particularly exciting is that over time, as adoption of the platform grows and the community's commitment to working together in this way expands, this use of the most advanced technologies will continue its own ability to learn from each individual action taken, by each individual user, and become better and better at guiding users toward the specific actions needed to move us collectively forward. In this way, the technology helps each of us achieve our own individual goals more quickly and rebuilds entire supply chains in the process!

Implementing SustainChain

Next I'll share how the SustainChain technology platform was implemented. As mentioned above, there is tremendous innovation, investment, and effort currently happening around the world focused on huge and existential problems, like the risks presented by climate change. Thousands, if not millions, of people work tirelessly toward this goal, with the intention of having an impact on the problem in a meaningful way. Applying the framework to a gargantuan problem like the fragility of global supply chains allowed me to highlight the playbook's immense power to cut through layers and layers of challenging issues and complexity, and show you how a *white space* solution like the SustainChain platform can emerge and be sketched out as a direct result of this framework and process.

white space, n.: A term used to describe a solution that has heretofore escaped our discovery, or has not yet been successfully implemented.

SustainChain is also an excellent example of a situation where technology greatly enables one to discover solutions to a highly complex problem, despite lacking expertise in any of its many granular aspects. In this case, the changemaker playbook process was used to reflect on things affecting the vulnerability of our global supply chains. I then engaged in a gap analysis that compared the fragmented nature of existing efforts with the changes required to make them function with resilience in the future state. These steps, just like the other examples shared, led me to uncover an innovative way for technology to address the underlying issues—rapidly, intelligently, and holistically.

Using the Gap Analysis to Test Hypotheses

The next step is no doubt now very familiar to you: I utilized the refinement cycle to challenge the efficacy and viability of the actions suggested by the gap analysis. You know that your plan for taking action must be flexible, and give you the ability to adjust for roadblocks and avoid blind alleys. In this regard, it was critical for me to think about how to build a platform for such a massive and highly fragmented ecosystem in a way that could increase the likelihood that organizations would discover, join, and use the platform. Therefore, I challenged the idea of building the Sustain Chain platform in this way before starting to implement it.

The first and most important thing that needed to be considered was what might prevent people from embracing the value of a platform like SustainChain to support their efforts or to become a part of the holistic community it was designed to foster. Our main hypothesis was that the platform first and foremost would need to be easy to use—a "no-brainer"—this bar remained at the very heart of how SustainChain was built from the start. We also believed that users would need to instantly feel that they are in a safe and trusted place, free from bad actors, and that they are able to work in a setting that would prevent unequal influence from forming in some part of the community.

In order to achieve this objective and make the future state vision possible, we began designing a user environment where each member, regardless of their area of focus in sustainability, could quickly and easily become part of a broader community of their peers. This was a high-priority task given that adding what feels like extra work to an already onerous set of tasks is rightly perceived to be the opposite of helpful. We answered for this by making these changemakers visible to one another and highlighting opportunities to succeed with their work faster together. That begins with a simple onboarding to the platform whereby the user provides a small set of basic, high-level details regarding the focus of their work (e.g., water security, renewable energy, regenerative agriculture); the role they play in their work (e.g., impact investor, researcher, technology innovator/entrepreneur, supply chain provider); the industries they work within or across (e.g., consumer products, financial services, energy); and where they are located geographically. Each of these questions is prompted automatically by the system, which provides the user with a standard set of options to choose from. As part of making the steps as quick and easy as possible, we even set ourselves the challenge of building it so that it required the least number of keystrokes possible (see Figures 5.2–5.4).

The information provided by users during the onboarding step of joining SustainChain allows each to instantly become part of one broad-based and holistic community dedicated to supply chain resiliency (see Figure 5.5). The technology platform immediately thereafter begins to provide recommendations to users on ways to bridge the gaps that would otherwise separate them from one another. SustainChain was built specifically to spot similar attributes among members, highlight what they share in common—whether taking similar actions or totally different ones—and to make the opportunities to collaborate known to them. Without this capability, these groups might never become aware of the opportunities to work together and potentially combine their resources and efforts (see Figure 5.6).

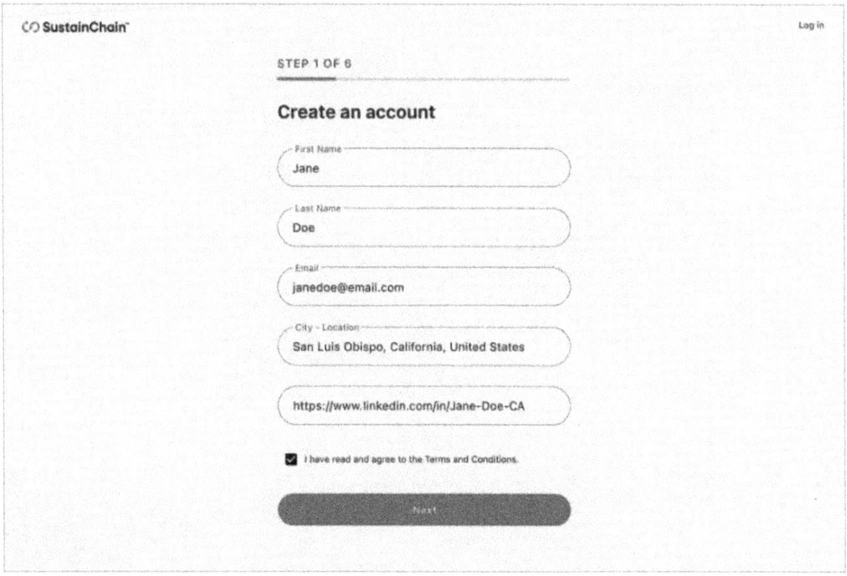

Figure 5.2   SustainChain account creation form.

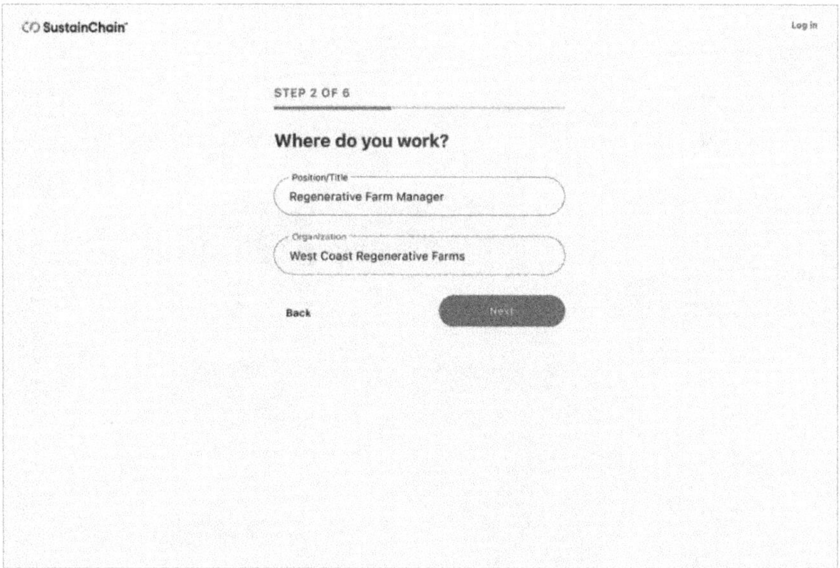

Figure 5.3   Provide details about your industry and your position in it.

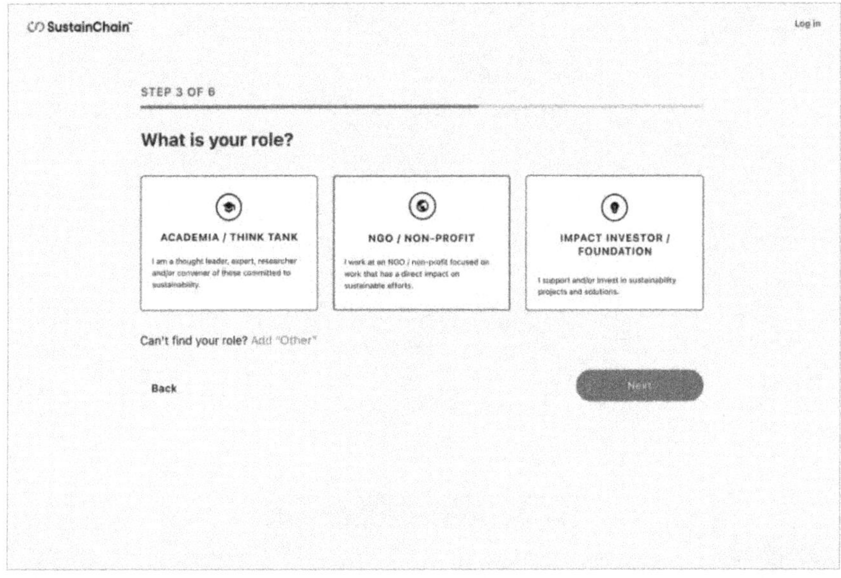

Figure 5.4   Select your role in the industry provided in the previous question.

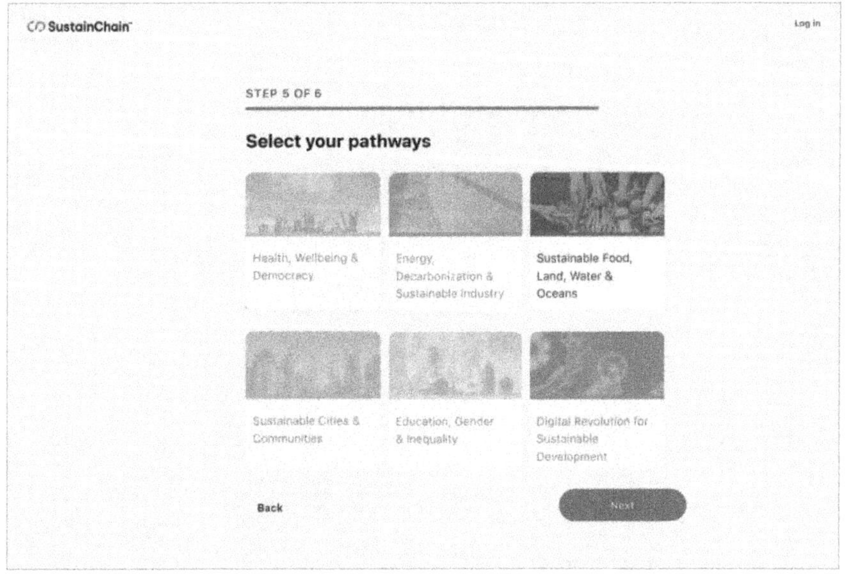

Figure 5.5   Select the sustainability pathways you are working on.

Figure 5.6   The option to select the UN Sustainable Development Goals (SDGs) you most identify with.

Being a member of the SustainChain community provides access to whole new sets of tools and resources that can help advance progress on the work, and in this sense becomes a safe and neutral public utility. Figure 5.7 shows a personalized SustainChain home page. Once you're a member, the platform is built to take you on a guided journey that connects you to the user community based on how relevant other members' work is to yours.

Anyone who uses Google or the latest chatbot or AI agent is familiar with its easy search and prompt capability, and that same type of feature is available on SustainChain—and since SustainChain is constantly learning through its reinforcement learning layer, it additionally provides recommended actions, solutions, and other members that might contribute to your work. These are all presented on your own personal home page, not dissimilar to what you might find on any one of your favorite social network platforms (this is not accidental, as you'll learn in Chapter 10).

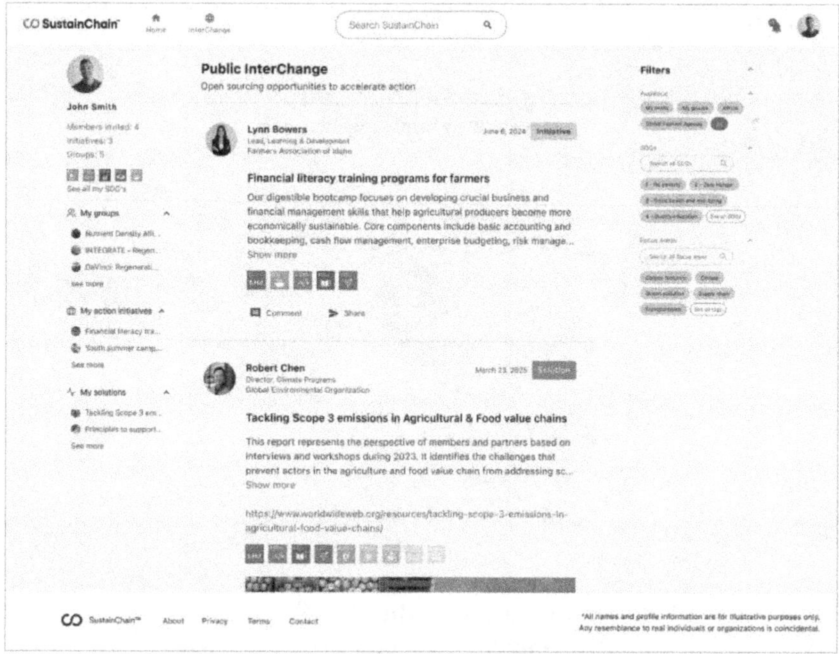

Figure 5.7   Your personalized SustainChain home page.

Using SustainChain to Connect to Others

Remember, SustainChain is ultimately built to help achieve a future state that ensures sustainable sources of water, food, and energy, which relies on the overarching need to build resilient global supply chains. Consider a member of the community that is focused on the particular area of regenerative farming, for instance. SustainChain connects them to others within their own group or organization, who may be working within separate areas but on similar tasks (see Figures 5.8–5.10).

Rebuilding global supply chains will of course require huge collections of individuals across industries and the globe to be successful. Achieving world scale won't be easy. Part of the difficulty of moving the individual work already underway forward lies in an ability to swiftly secure the correct resources, tools, and partnerships. Another major challenge we have is keeping the efforts that are occurring coordinated within and across the large number of people already working together within their respective companies or organizations.

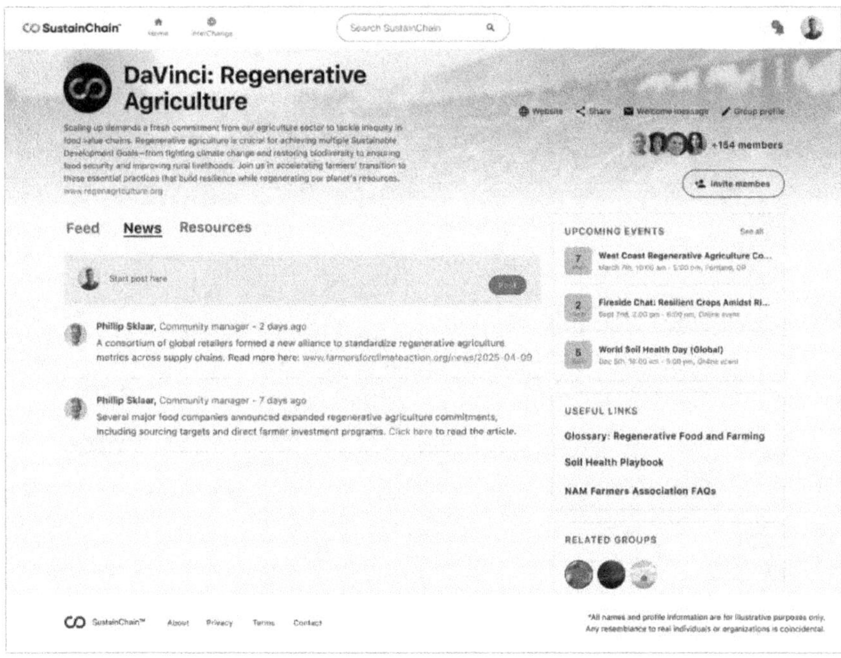

Figure 5.8 The action portal newsfeed.

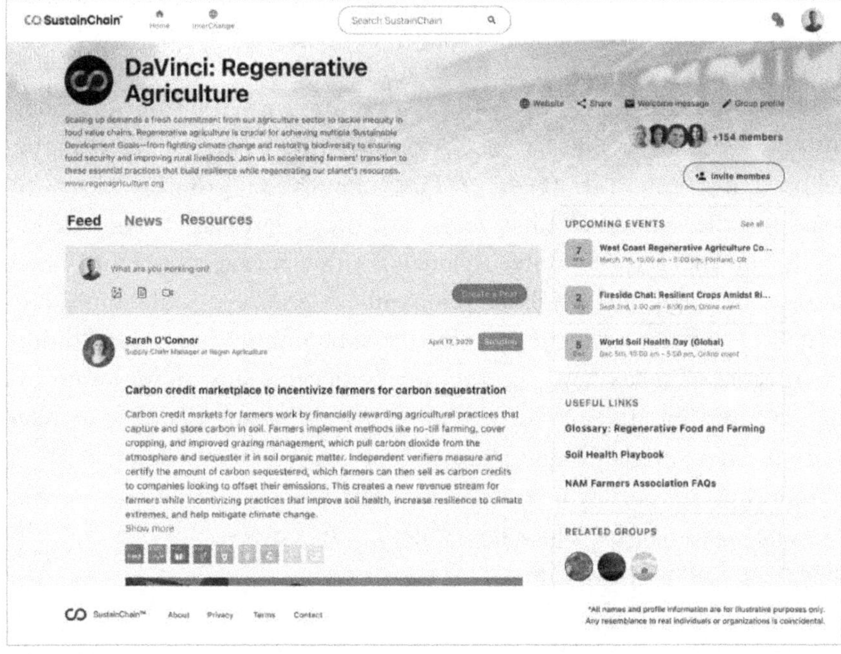

Figure 5.9 Posts created and shared for this pathway are shown in the Feed tab.

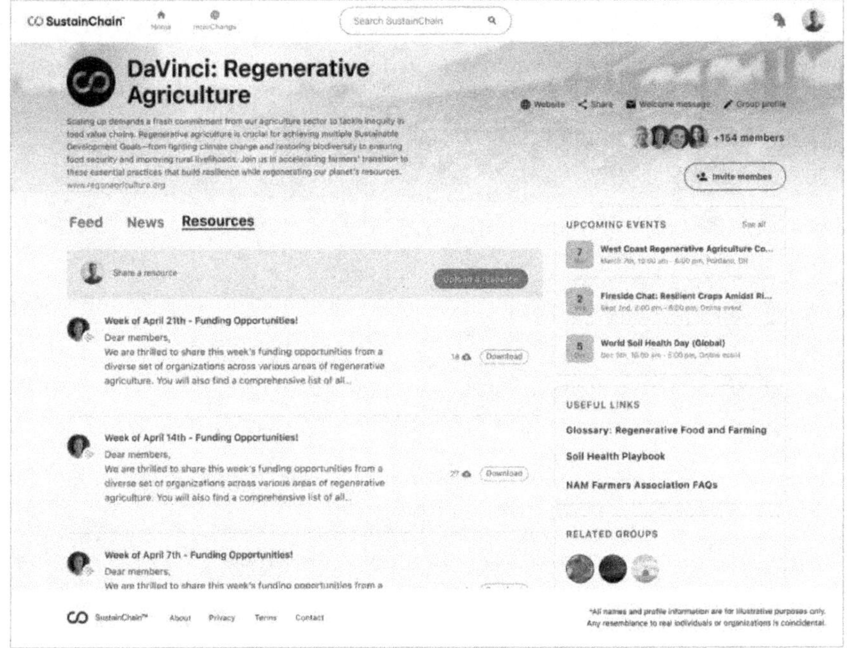

Figure 5.10 Resources for a given pathway are shown in the Resources tab.

SustainChain addresses this by providing a space within the technology platform, not just for connecting individuals but for bringing whole subcommunities together. This allows these groups to instantly combine the actions of the people and organizations working within them, and make them more organized, efficient, and impactful. Then, just as it does for individual members *within* a subcommunity, SustainChain also identifies things that subcommunities of one industry or area of focus have in common with *other* subcommunities and their action initiatives. This, as before, brings instant visibility to relevant partnerships and opportunities to collaborate that exist. It's a potent way to grow those networks and secure missing pieces (like funding), to solve for blockages together, or combine efforts for efficiency and effectiveness in order to scale faster.

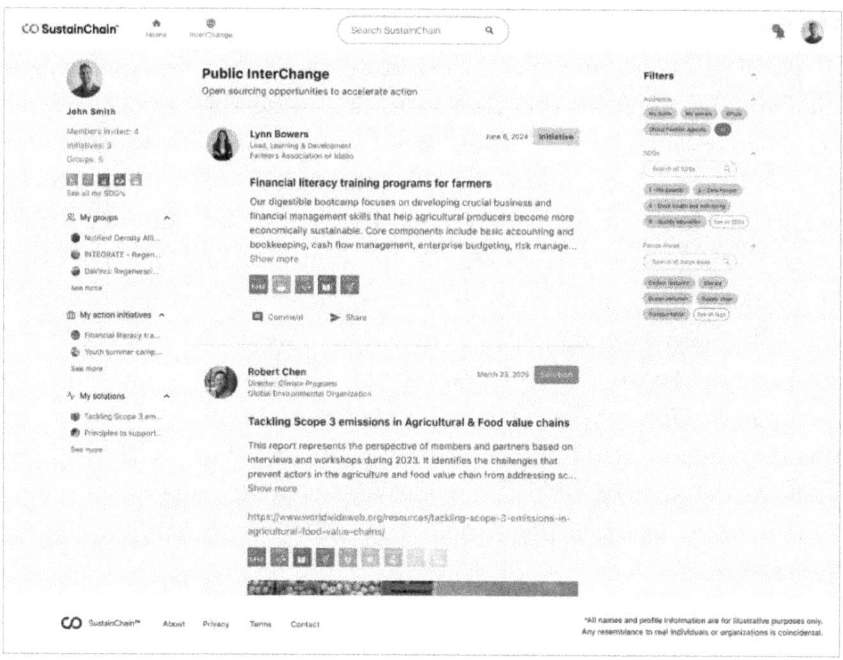

Figure 5.11   The SustainChain Interchange.

To complement the automated way that the platform reveals opportunities and suggests action initiatives that members or groups might not be aware of, SustainChain is built to also be a central place where members share new opportunities with the entire community (see Figure 5.11).

Figure 5.11 shows the SustainChain Interchange, where members can offer or request a product, service, or technology from their organization, or refer a skill or talent they think others in the community may benefit from. The post can be shared publicly with the entire member community, or with subcommunities, or groups of members as shown in Figures 5.8–5.10, where members are focused on a common area like regenerative agriculture.

Creating a Mission Control

As a final part of sharing how the playbook was used to attack the biggest stumbling blocks, it became clear to us that being able to "see" what is being accomplished on the whole, at any moment in time, will be just as critical. This is a key input to the refinement cycle aspect of our process because it allows for the highest response times to the guidance it provides. The point here is that even if you can successfully build a platform like SustainChain, and it leads to creating the largest and most cohesive and collaborative community of changemakers ever, knowing how far you are traveling toward the future state is what allows you to adjust the plan accordingly. This is where taking another page from the book of our friends at NASA came in—a Mission Control was built to dynamically visualize the sum of all the individualized actions being taken within SustainChain! Figure 5.12 provides a snapshot of the Mission Control home screen.

mission control, n.: A centralized hub for monitoring, coordinating, and directing complex operations to ensure successful outcomes.

For a solution like SustainChain visualizing the whole becomes as important as effort itself for a changemaker. And the solution? You guessed it—technology. Applying development tools from a select number of coding languages and software tools, a Mission Control was built that allows members a way to view the sum total of the numerous simultaneous efforts being taken from all different angles. This capability provides unique insight into what the community is accomplishing, where it is making relative progress together, and, as importantly, where it is not. It's a unique capability in that it can highlight both the gaps and opportunities that exist across industries and supply chains, and be: a source of solutions with fresh applications, geographic expansion opportunities, and expertise being—all generated by actions occurring or a use case being deployed member or group on the chain not yet part of the community's collective work (see Figures 5.13 and 5.14).

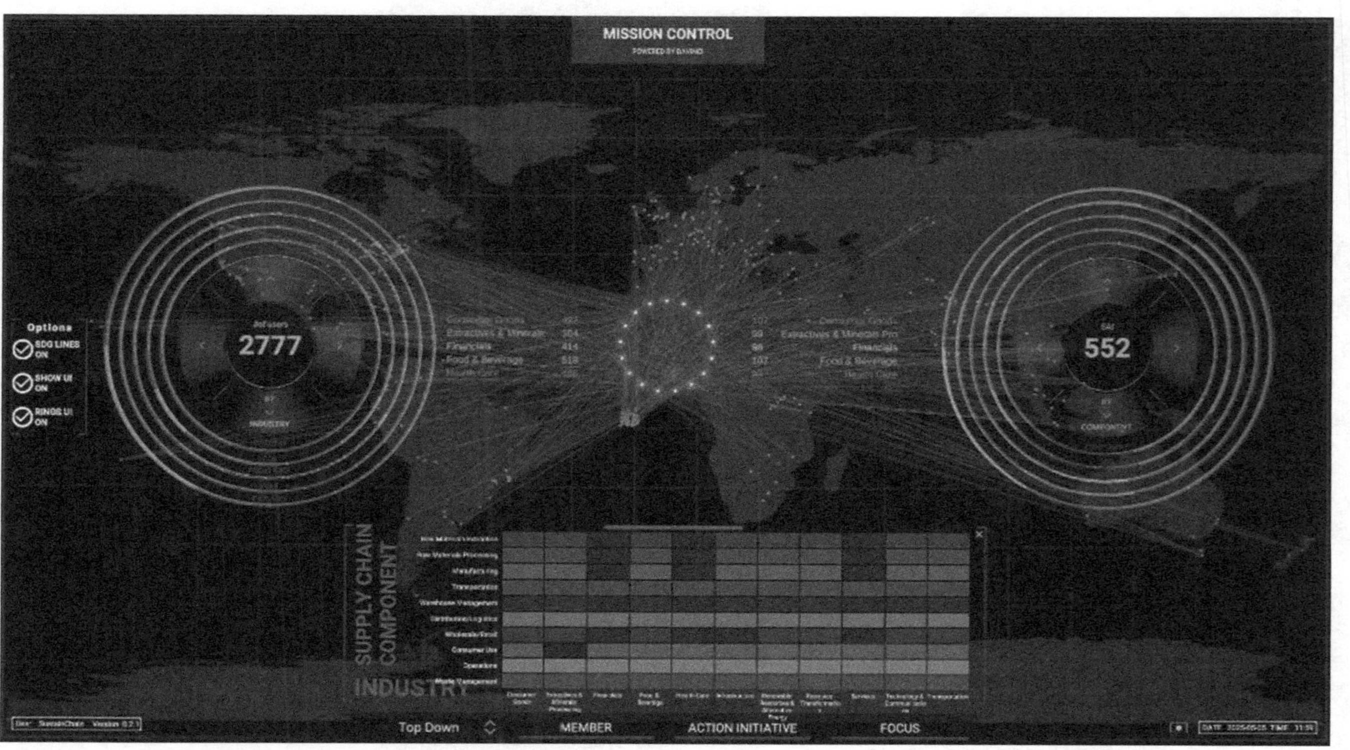

Figure 5.12   Mission Control home screen.

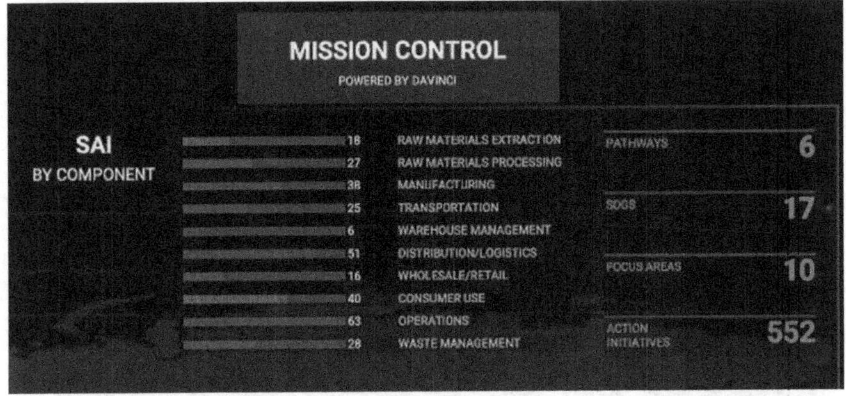

Figure 5.13   Mission Control's display of sustainability action initiatives taking place across the platform.

Figure 5.14   Mission Control also keeps track of the number of its members, companies, and groups in each industry.

Key Takeaways

The SustainChain journey shared with you in this chapter illustrates the way technology was applied to provide a novel platform that helps changemakers move past paralyzing complexity and the immense number of issues faced when confronting global food, water, and energy security challenges. The platform accomplishes this by combining digital software, internet capabilities, and machine learning. Together, these technologies make the *how* for successfully rebuilding global supply chains across industries appear possible. They also bring the much needed transparency, organization, connection, and real-time guidance that allows SustainChain to be a neutral space, where individuals and working groups can stay focused on their own goals and objectives, while the platform dynamically suggests ways to address critical resource gaps and partnership needs among them. Members from organizations of all sizes and types are now part of a protected, expanding digital community that benefits collectively from the individual actions of each and all.

While SustainChain's creation may have been a novel one, the idea behind it was not. This is true even for my personal discovery process—and, in fact, it's mostly common sense. It's just another example of what can happen when you are able to think about a problem differently, and use deep, structured, and creative thinking. It shows you how doing so can shine fresh light on the real issues behind massive challenges, like securing a future where humanity's basic needs to survive—like water, food, and energy—and suggest the "hows" for plugging in missing pieces.

This chapter once again focuses on the pivotal role of the changemaker playbook process as a reliable way to keep your thoughts clear and organized when taking on problems of any kind or size, and to prioritize the relevant actions necessary to push toward the future state defined in each. The SustainChain example illustrates once again how the playbook process, supported by modern technology, reliably identifies productive and efficient ways to take action—enabling the doing.

(continued)

(*continued*)

Where reinforcing the resilience of global supply chains is specifically concerned, SustainChain illustrates how the process leads to practical and scalable ways to take organized holistic action. In this case, it also makes doing the business of change more efficient and thus less costly in terms of time, investment, and effort. There is a natural logic to it—in other words, it just *makes sense*. It provides a neutral action hub, accessible by all who can extract value from it, with no hidden costs, gimmicks, or barriers to entry beyond the need for a phone or laptop, a genuine commitment and the drive to get started.

In this example I isolated the goal of securing basic human needs by rebuilding global supply chains, to illustrate the ways technology becomes essential to your success when pursuing big change. It highlights the critical role of technology for getting and staying on a faster track to impact on a world level. SustainChain's design illustrates how our human ability to take actions of this magnitude will most definitely rely in large part on the proper and adequate use of the most advanced available technologies. And, in the case of climate resilience and sustainability, for which we face an urgent timetable for success, technology will also be required to achieve whatever we can, however we can, at top speed.

This sets the perfect stage for a deeper exploration of the role and potential of machine learning and artificial intelligence (AI) in a quest to effect important change in a short timeframe. You are about to see how the learning capabilities embedded at the core of SustainChains become one with its utility and unique value in rebuilding global supply chains—quickly.

6

Ethical AI: Maximum Impact Potential at Top Speed

In the previous chapter, you had the opportunity to view the changemaker playbook process in action and technology's vital place in it. I shared examples with you from my personal journey, beginning with the Signet customer experience where the company designed a future state to rebuild every one of its businesses, products, and services around one leading edge customer technology platform. And then I walked through the "clean sheet" creation of a platform called SustainChain to illustrate technology's massive utility to the large and growing community of sustainability changemakers. In the case of SustainChain, the platform is a literal example of building an engine for achieving personal impact using technology as both a tool and overall solution for overcoming complexity.

When sketching it out on my clean sheet of paper, SustainChain seemed like a great idea, but it was making proper use of bleeding-edge technology that provided the route to creating a digital home for confronting the effects of climate change on global supply chains. Technology was the source of leverage we needed to follow through on our intention to take meaningful action, with measurable success.

In this chapter, I build further on the SustainChain story to highlight the magnitude of potential you can create when you use cutting-edge technologies wherever possible, and in particular, the unique role of artificial intelligence (AI) in that process. Among other things, I will review AI's special power and explain how it can feed your conviction that conquering world-scale problems at top speed is both doable *and* manageable.

Stepping Back

As noted last chapter SustainChain first emerged by focusing on what's called white space, what was missing. You'll recall from the definition provided that a white space solution is one that has not yet been successfully implemented.

These solutions can actually be found almost anywhere. The particular white space that SustainChain occupies lies in the purposeful way it is designed in order to facilitate progress on efforts to rebuild supply chains. Because we defined the future state as one where all parts of the supply chain in every industry would operate in a resilient and cohesive manner, redesigned to reinforce one another, we were able to focus on how to leverage technology in order to make both of these a practical reality.

One part of reducing the fragmented nature of efforts seeking to address these issues was developing a capability that would:

- Chip away at their often isolated, or "silo-driven" nature
- Provide support to actions focused on the unique aspects of the future state
- Nudge those who are working on common challenges to join forces, creating a *1 + 1 = 3 effect*.

1 + 1 = 3 effect, n.: An idiom referring to the synergistic relationship of two forces.

For these reasons, SustainChain became a technology platform purpose-built to foster a holistic community of changemakers across all industries, supply chains, and sustainability priorities. It's a live example of how technology can be used in a highly specific way to address the unique parts of solving a problem and lead us toward the most effective paths. When utilized in very targeted and deliberate ways like this, technology can help erase some of the obstacles that prevent us from making progress and, as importantly, reveal completely new opportunities to address problems that might not surface on their own. These things, as well as the crucial ability to dramatically elevate the personal impact we can potentially achieve, cannot be overstated in urgent situations like the future of our planet, where we truly need all hands on deck.

Technology gives SustainChain its unique advantage to simultaneously advance individual progress as well as that of the whole. It also provides another critical bit of help. World-scale problems like climate resilience not only require highly coordinated actions among a sea of groups and individuals, but they often also have the added difficulty of manifesting solutions on a strict deadline. In other words, speed can ultimately make or break the chances that you succeed in achieving the change and impact that's needed, *fast enough*. Broadly speaking, digitization and the internet are the very backbone of creating tools and solutions that match that urgency. For a utility like SustainChain, the hyper speed that its software can enable sets it apart, made possible by the specific use of AI.

Before I dive more deeply into how AI was specifically applied to build a supply chain resiliency solution, it will help to first take a step back and ground your understanding of what we refer to when we discuss AI in the context of the past.

Humans have a history of developing new and more sophisticated tools to compensate for the pitfalls of older strategies, for solutions in anything from business to agriculture. I share just a few of these examples from the last few decades, in the realm of digitization and computer programming. These examples also involve companies and industries that now utilize AI as the logical next step to continuing to innovate solutions. Not only has digital technology been utilized (and in some cases made more sophisticated) for the specific purpose of solving an apparent problem, but this practice often culminates in the genesis of AI.

The aim is to instill in you the mindset that proactively seeking to replicate this approach—that is, utilizing the latest technology to design a suitable solution to most any problem—is an *essential tool* for maximizing your own personal impact. It is also to reassure you that, while you may feel a little out of your depth when it comes to understanding bleeding-edge technologies like AI, the courage and drive to forge ahead and test the limits of new technology to achieve the biggest impact possible is a part of our shared history as human beings.

Sophisticated Solutions: Lessons from the Past

In a relatively short period of about 10 years or so, digital and internet technologies reached a new level of power. They help us see the bigger picture more clearly, execute numerous complex tasks far more easily, and do both things simultaneously rather than sequentially.

It began with the entry of digital technologies (in the form of tools, devices, and systems used to process, store, and communicate information), and was followed by the emergence of internet capabilities that mushroomed practically without pause since the World Wide Web emerged more than 30 years ago. This created a unique opportunity in human history to revolutionize practically every industry, beginning with (now commonplace) rules-based software, and culminating eventually in the development of AI.

As far as examples, the world of business is perhaps the most obvious place to begin. After all, AI has become all but ubiquitous in businesses the world over, and business tools utilizing AI are now transforming entire industries by making production more efficient, less costly, and more flexible, among other things. But before AI, businesses were arguably first in line to use the latest technology to forge ahead of the competition, especially after digital technology and the internet became commonplace. There are several software solutions, for example, that were used before the emergence of AI that allowed companies to innovate new avenues for efficiency, automation, expansion, and profitability. We have benefited from these solutions as a society, in one way or another, for much longer than the latest advances in AI became standard—often in interesting ways we may overlook or take for granted.

For example, in 1964, airlines began automating their operations by developing a tool to improve the processing time of airline reservations and ticketing, manage flight schedules and availability, and enhance customer service and support. The so-called "Sabre System" was developed by a partnership of US companies American Airlines (AA) and IBM, and it revolutionized the airline industry as the first centralized airline reservation system (IBM, n.d.). Before Sabre, handwritten cards were used to keep track of customer flight information—imagine that! After Sabre, AA computers around the country were linked together in one centralized network, cutting a previous reservation processing time of 90 minutes to just a few seconds.

The massive improvements in efficiency and productivity created by the system were a major breakthrough—with reservation time greatly reduced, booking speed grew exponentially, and overbooking and underbooking errors were reduced substantially as well. It's safe to say that without a software solution like this one, it might still be commonplace to book all plane tickets with a live representative. This was just the beginning of a turning point in business, at the time tailor-made for the airline industry, that would generate exciting advances in the customer experience. Sabre made real-time availability and automated booking confirmations possible. Now, AI chatbots and virtual assistants are integrated into the AA reservation experience, building on the tailor-made software solutions of decades before to advance the customer experience even further (McCann, 2025).

In a different industry—one that ties in nicely with the resiliency discussion last chapter—the emergence of precision agriculture coincided with developments in computerization and digital software. With the development of the world economy and the historic rise of the global population in recent decades, the demand for food has likewise increased on a scale unprecedented in human history, and new difficulties are routinely encountered in the need to farm efficiently. The average person never considers the sheer amount of data analysis that goes into modern agriculture—there are dozens of factors to monitor, measure, and take into account at any given moment, from soil variation in different geographic locations, to unfavorable weather patterns, to the potential spread of bacterial illnesses, to the insect resistance of different kinds of crops (Cecere, 2023).

Understandably, this makes feeding the world a somewhat difficult task. In the past, analysis of all these factors could take days at a time, creating a slow, tedious, inefficient system for the expansion of the industry. This would all be transformed with the advent of computer-assisted farming in the 1980s, with the creation of digital agricultural resource maps and the introduction of computer-aided farming (CAF), which could, for example, translate geographic and spatial information into fertilizer application maps (Haneklaus, Lilienthal, and Schnug, 2016). The speed of data processing in agriculture effectively boomed, and as I demonstrate in the following section, continues to be streamlined with the utilization of AI in the same areas. Precision agricultural technologies have been widespread ever since.

With these examples of computerization transforming a couple of different industries, the next section moves on to a more detailed exploration of how ethical AI is being used to propel humans toward making groundbreaking advances.

Ethical AI: An Overview

> *ethical AI,* n.: Artificial intelligence systems that prioritize fairness, accountability, transparency, and privacy, ensuring they benefit society and minimize harm and bias.

As mentioned, since it emerged the internet has enabled a massive global network of interconnected computers and servers that rapidly exchange information and, in turn, generate online communication and information sharing. In addition, humans have witnessed the creation of an array of digital resources and other tools, ones that we now utilize every day. The ability to make our lives simpler and more productive, as well as to push the limits of our creativity, has been helped in countless ways by both digitization and the internet that we don't often reflect on.

More recently, these technologies have been taken to an exponentially new level with the ascendance of AI. Most experts—if not all—operating in various fields of AI believe its capabilities have cleared many new thresholds for transforming our lives and the world, in ways that make it virtually impossible to ignore.

> *artificial intelligence (AI),* n.: A vast field of digital tool development utilizing computer systems that are designed to perform complex tasks normally done by human reasoning, decision-making, creating, and so on.

Because of the way it seemed to burst onto the scene with little to no warning, the shift in mindset that AI feeds felt sudden for many. However, computer programming itself was something of a precursor to AI and is far from new. Indeed, many of what we now know to be predecessors of the AI we use today had been used for many decades. The interest in creating a computer that could complete tasks normally done by human reasoning has existed for several decades, and you can see some examples of these throughout history. One of these first entered the public domain in the late 1950s: a computer program called the Logic Theorist (LT).

The Beginning: The Advent of LT

LT is a helpful example to reflect on, given its early capabilities to use computational models to simulate human problem-solving abilities. Developed in 1956 by Allen Newell and Herbert Simon, it used logical deduction to reason about simple problems, and both explore possible solutions and find the most appropriate one. LT's objective was to demonstrate the feasibility of simulating human cognition, which is also a fundamental factor of the direction that modern AI has taken. It was only in the 2010s that the term "AI" made its way into mainstream conversations, and in the early 2020s, it suddenly became difficult to go practically anywhere without hearing the two letters.

To help clarify the breadth of AI's present capacity to support our ability to take personal action with impact, it is helpful to explore a range of practical examples.

Some Relatable Examples

Let's start in an area that touches many lives either directly or indirectly every day, by looking at the medical field. AI algorithms are commonly used, for instance, to analyze medical images such as CT and MRI scans, which are typically used to check for injuries and health conditions not easily visible on the surface.

> *algorithm,* n.: A series of steps or instructions designed to solve a problem or complete a process. In technology, these instructions are given to a computer for tasks like opening an application, sorting a list of documents, or increasing the brightness on your screen.

The immense value of algorithms lies in their capability to improve on the time and accuracy of diagnosing medical conditions such as heart disease and cancer.

For example, a study from May 2022 found that the AI could detect small growths in the lung faster and with a similar or better accuracy than an experienced radiologist. It also found 8.4 percent more than experts with the naked eye. To quote the study, "When aided by AI, the expert decreased the average assessment time per case from 2:44 minutes to 35.7 seconds, while reporting an overall increase in confidence" (Abadia et al., 2022).

AI has also helped in drug discovery. Rentosertib is considered the very *first* AI-developed drug. Developed by a company called Insilico Medicine to treat a condition called idiopathic pulmonary fibrosis (IPF), it is the first drug where both the target (the molecules specifically linked to the disease) (Santos et al., 2016) and the compound (the mix of chemicals with the potential to treat the disease) were discovered using generative AI. Though not yet available to the wider public, it is on track to be cleared for widespread public consumption as of this writing (Drug Target Review, 2025).

If you consider all these examples together, you begin to get a fuller sense of AI's ability to decode complexity and supercharge efficiency. Imagine the potential these technologies now hold to redefine entire fields of science, medicine, and business.

A Powerful Means for Rapid Discovery of New Paths

In the specific context of the changemaker playbook, this section explores AI's ability to leap beyond these types of benefits, to create whole new paths for making personal impact—perhaps even new futures.

You'll recall from the last chapter that it was through incorporating AI into SustainChain's digital and internet-enabled backbone that we were able to instantly shift our actions into overdrive. It's the only way to generate personalized guidance at the speed we will inevitably need to win the race against climate. By taking full advantage, and with a little luck on our own timing for doing so, ethical AI can literally help us beat the clock.

Ethical AI, responsible AI, or "AI for good," is a fast-growing field that can accelerate the progress toward resiliency, and hopefully make the prospects for moving fast enough less scary over time. Used responsibly and deliberately, AI can help create completely new paths to rapid, informed, practical action with immense potential that are literally hiding in plain sight.

While rebuilding global supply chains has a huge number of moving parts, AI algorithms have advanced far beyond the baby steps taken 10 years ago; they now have the potential to accelerate regenerative agriculture efforts in many remarkable ways.

Take, for instance, this pest and disease warning system. Developed by the Dabeinong Group, this AI and big data system analyzes real-time crop growth data and environmental conditions to predict the likelihood of pest and disease outbreaks. It also issues timely warnings to guide farmers on implementing appropriate preventive measures. This system has already improved pest and disease control efficiency over the numerous agricultural bases it now covers by 20 percent (Ding and Gao, 2025).

Similarly, the Beidahuang Group employs drones and sensors for soil and crop monitoring, using AI algorithms to analyze the data and provide precise fertilization and irrigation plans. Statistics show that this technology has increased Beidahuang Group's water resource utilization by 36 percent and crop yield by 5 percent. Incorporating AI into agricultural systems offers the potential to address key agricultural challenges, enhance sustainability, and promote global food security. Predictive analytics analyzes data such as soil and weather conditions, crop yield, and plant health, and provides farmers with real-time insights they can use to optimize crop rotations, determine ideal planting times, and reduce waste in the water and fertilizer used. These steps simultaneously increase agricultural yields and reduce negative impacts on land quality.

AI-powered drones and satellites monitor crop growth, and they can identify potential problems, such as pest infestations or nutrient deficiencies, much earlier. With these tools, farmers can address issues like these before they escalate and damage crops, which leads to more sustainable and efficient farming practices. AI-powered precision farming tools, such as variable-rate fertilization and irrigation systems, allow farmers to customize and optimize their farming methods, by applying water and nutrients precisely where they are needed. Doing so optimizes their ability to reduce waste and prevent overapplication of fertilizers, pesticides, and the like, thereby reducing their negative environmental effects.

AI technologies are assessing overall soil health, as well. They can analyze data from sensors and imaging technology. Among other benefits, this allows farmers to identify nutrient deficiencies and soil erosion. This will lead to increasingly healthy crops and more sustainable farming practices.

In addition to these farming examples, certain advanced forms of AI are also being used to dramatically eliminate plastic waste from industry supply chains. The Global Plastic Watch platform (GPW), for instance, uses the first-ever reliable methodology to detect and monitor trends in plastic pollution on land, and in near real time (Minderoo Foundation, 2017). It is a novel decision and management support tool for plastic waste that has been developed with the goal of stopping plastic waste *before* it enters the ocean. GPW leverages free and publicly available satellite imagery from the European Space Agency, as well as the latest advances in machine learning. It detects the locations of plastic waste dumpsites and aggregation sites on land. GPW monitors and reports on the trends in the size of the plastic waste sites.

Similarly, there are several related ways AI can contribute to the negative impact of the fashion supply chain on water and land. This is particularly important, because the global fashion industry is responsible for approximately 20 percent of the world's water contamination. In other words, one-fifth of contaminated water globally can be traced back to fashion-related activities, like textile dyeing, finishing, and the chemicals used in processing fabrics. The impact includes the release of toxic chemicals, heavy metals, and microfibers into water systems, affecting our environmental and human health. Here are a few ways AI algorithms are being used to confront these issues:

- Material traceability uses real-time data analytics to track both the *source and journey* of the materials used in fashion, from production to usage and disposal, to increase the efficiency of efforts to reduce waste and recycling efforts within the industry.

- An array of other sustainability analytics is used to analyze the environmental *impact* of fashion products, using the data generated to identify ways to refine supply chains and reduce the environmental footprint.
- Textile waste is intelligently sorted, which reduces the amount that ends up in landfills and enables the industry to move toward a more circular model. One AI-powered sorting machine, for example, sorts up to 10 tons of clothing per week, using spectral sensors and image analysis to simultaneously sort textiles across various locations (Clubley, 2025).

And in this final group, critical of course to sustainably rebuilding global supply chains, is fossil fuel reduction, where the number of ways to improve efficiency, consumption, and waste is rapidly growing. Here are some examples:

- AI-powered smart grids can manage the modern electrical grid by balancing energy production and consumption. These solutions allow the grid to optimize fossil fuel energy, and wherever possible integrate new renewable energy sources, in real time.
- AI is constantly improving industrial efficiency in manufacturing processes, reducing energy consumption and pollution to optimize and reduce usage.
- AI-powered predictive models are continually improving the accuracy of climate modeling.
- Perhaps most exciting of all, AI is used to create cleaner fuel and harness renewable energy sources such as solar, wind, nuclear, and hydro. It does this by forecasting energy demand and providing new ways to make consumption across all these sources more accessible and efficient.

This wide range of cases, where AI is being used in both groundbreaking and responsible ways, provides a rich context for understanding AI's unique ability to rapidly iterate and adapt. Its vast potential also offers a continuously growing source of creativity that shows things through a completely different lens. Like Newton did, we can see the same things differently, make new discoveries, and execute new approaches with agility and precision.

Perhaps it is even easier to see, when taken all together, how the discussion thus far also shines a bright light on why AI sits at the core of SustainChain's unique capabilities. The next section discusses this in more depth to explain why this became so.

Creating DaVinci

At the heart of SustainChain's design is a hypothesis that fully harnessing the capabilities of AI can transform the platform into a uniquely powerful and consequential enabler of resilient supply chains. That is, by taking advantage of its capacity to exponentially cut the time to take informed action, align and combine the individual actions of its members, and fill partnership and resource needs, we can turbocharge our collective progress. That's why a highly specific set of AI capabilities were combined to build the DaVinci Discovery Engine (DDE).

> *Leonardo DaVinci,* personal n.: Innovator, architect, scientist, and one of the most influential artists in history. He left a legacy of groundbreaking contributions in the realms of art, math, science, and architecture, each discipline informing his mastery of the others.

DaVinci was the name chosen for SustainChain's AI engine because discovering pathways to the transformational change needed must be informed by each of the disciplines that are required to rebuild global supply chains, and because an AI capability that succeeds in this way can potentially lead to the creation of whole new futures.

Recall the DaVinci Discovery Engine's main job. It is designed to guide organizations of different sizes and types toward one another's work, as well as give them access to the critical resources, innovations, partnerships, and funding sources that are essential to achieving their goals. DaVinci looks dynamically and continuously for missing pieces that can advance the progress of the work happening across the entire SustainChain community, from the relevant to the instrumental. And because this is the only job the machine has, it also becomes an accelerator that provides every opportunity it spots at the highest pace possible.

> *elixir,* n.: A catalyst or essential force that energizes and accelerates progress.

Chapter 5 touched on the importance of making the actions that take place on the platform visible to the community at all times. Part of the point established there is that even if SustainChain becomes the largest, most comprehensive and collaborative global community of changemakers in the world, we will also need to know whether, how far, and how quickly we are traveling toward the future state. We need this, of course, if we are to know where we are actually making the right type of progress and whether we are making it fast enough.

I also shared the tool that was built to understand this, called Mission Control. As described previously, Mission Control allows members of the SustainChain community to visualize the sum of all the interrelated actions taking place. It was also designed to reflect members' relative progress—which industries, geographies, and organization types are progressing faster than others, and where there are opportunities for changemakers to build on one another's successes. DaVinci even suggests paths to unlock progress in one industry or supply chain for the benefit of another. For example, consider an advanced solution to address water contamination that creates progress for resilient farming practices, as well as reduces chemicals released in the manufacturing process in the fashion industry. This is called *spillover*.

> *spillover,* n.: The unintended transfer or impact of effects from one context, activity, or system to another.

Mission Control's ability to bring visibility in all these ways and to cause spillover is made possible by the DaVinci Discovery Engine. DaVinci is constantly learning from every action by every individual impacting every supply chain in a positive way. It does so by identifying what members have in common, sometimes because of spillover effects from another individual or organization, tool, resource, or partnership.

This capability has been created by using a particular form of AI called *reinforcement learning* (RL). Reinforcement learning is an area of AI with its earliest roots in the 1950s and 1960s, and as with many other early examples like LT, began to advance beyond its computational limitations. It was not until the 1980s that researchers laid the foundation for what we now know as modern RL. In the late 1990s, reinforcement learning began to gain widespread attention due to major advances in its deep learning and computational power.

One of the most iconic examples of reinforcement learning AI, often used to explain its unique capacities, comes from an RL engine created by IBM's Deep Blue. Many know it as the computer that learned the game of chess from scratch and went on to beat chess grandmaster Gary Kasparov in 1997 (IBM, 2024). There were other examples of engines that followed the same basic approach as Deep Blue, like AlphaGo and AlphaZero. They are a combination of human-provided strategies and self-play to improve its game (Mucci, 2024). Google DeepMind's AlphaGo improved on Deep Blue by learning through a combination of supervised learning from human games and self-play to improve its strategy. AlphaZero was then created to learn entirely through self-play, utilizing a neural network and general-purpose algorithms that knew nothing about the game of chess but the basic rules (Silver et al., 2018). It also used a more advanced reinforcement learning algorithm that allowed it to discover novel strategies. *It was this feature of RL machine learning that led it to be chosen to become a major component of SustainChain's DaVinci Engine. Why?*

Embedding RL into the DaVinci learning engine builds on AI's natural enabling functions and streamlines, integrates, synthesizes, and directs the flow of intelligence. It does this by creating a comprehensive and definitive list of roles and expressed needs, which are summarized in Appendix A.

DaVinci represents the gateway to transformational change that SustainChain was built to provide. It allows you to amplify needed insight and fast-track actions, and it does so with transparency, a source of accountability, and new ways to apply technology innovation.

This example in Appendix A illustrates SustainChain members' work on ocean thermal energy (OTEC) as an alternative energy source: interactions among companies creating the capability and wherewithal to supply the energy systems that need to be built, the equipment required, the experts with the potential to construct the full solution, and the government support and business models to make it economically viable.

These activities are happening simultaneously, and the DaVinci learning engine is instantly revealing where connections lie and actions need to be made across SustainChain community members according to their roles and shared sustainability pathway focus. It also shows what members must prioritize to get to their goal by 2050. Regardless of whether we get there in a way that could be considered absolute, the machine helps systematically guide the actions still needed to work as a total end-to-end system. This example illustrates how the community stays informed and collaborates with each other to align, connect, and accelerate its actions.

DaVinci's task began with curating a member group with the common pathway focus to reduce the carbon footprint through offsets, alternative energy sources, and so on. Notifications linked to certain pathways, themes, and category actions were delivered to members as initiations occurred; early challenges and blockers alerted relevant members as they surfaced. Early outputs included the following:

- Alternative energy as the obvious long-term solution, of which there are many forms. Each has its own supply chain components or sub-components, but there is some overlap.
- Some supply chain components to expand the use of OTEC that might touch wind; solar is a key example.
- The insights shared can guide users investing in solar to potentially explore OTEC.

This systems-based guidance allows users to learn things they can't source anywhere else, because DaVinci connects those in SustainChain with what's happening within it and maps the characteristics of needed actions to the components that allow for the solution to become viable.

The success that DaVinci generates, then, happens by way of the unique mix of the data it collects and its ability to link, learn, and suggest new paths in a repeatable way. For a deeper understanding of DaVinci's capabilities and what makes it possible, refer to Appendix A.

Key Takeaways

As a part of sharing how the changemaker playbook process and my personal practice approach led to the "clean sheet of paper" design of SustainChain, I touched in Chapter 5 on the importance of being able to see what is being accomplished by the community. Part of the point being made was that even if SustainChain were to become the largest, most comprehensive, and collaborative global community of change-makers ever, we would also need to know whether and how far we have traveled toward the future state. We need this, of course, if we are to know where we are making progress and whether we are making it fast enough. Mission Control shows how SustainChain has been enabled to dynamically visualize the sum of all the interconnected actions taken.

This necessity of being able to see the big picture of our own efforts and the efforts of the entire community—in other words, the ability to visualize the whole—became a vital component of the plat-form. And the solution, once again: technology. By applying develop-ment tools from a select number of coding languages and software tools, we built the Mission Control tool to allow members to view the sum total of the numerous simultaneous efforts, when taken together and from all different angles, that gives unique insight to what the community is accomplishing, where it is making relative progress together, and where it is not. It has a unique ability to highlight even further the gaps and opportunities across whole industries and supply chains and generate solutions with fresh applications, as well as point out expansion opportunities in a new geographic region, or a new source of untapped potential not yet part of the collective work.

Independent of having a machine learning component, SustainChain would still be able to bring individuals into a holistic and organized community that is otherwise very challenging, and per-haps even impossible, to build manually. But applying ethically used AI uniquely boosts the power of SustainChain to give its community an ability to take quicker, more guided action, and to be dynamically informed on the gaps and opportunities that exist among them. Applied in this way, therefore, AI allows us to enter entirely new dimensions of innovation, enabling rapid advances in industries ranging from finance and agriculture to manufacturing and energy. All of this is pivotal to reaching the food, water, and energy security we hope to ensure in the future state.

Whether it's to design more efficient renewable energy grids, fine-tune climate models, or otherwise encourage sustainable behaviors, AI can supply important insight, tools, and other critical ingredients that can vastly accelerate our ability to take faster action and guide us toward data-driven decisions. This in turn provides us with an all-important opportunity to learn new ways to execute differently, more knowledgeably, and at a pace that can hopefully approach, if not match, the urgency of the challenges we face.

As you've seen now through the DaVinci Discovery Engine as well as the prior examples provided, AI has a highly unique ability to seamlessly merge speed with intelligence, and to radically expedite outcomes in virtually any field of human endeavor. It can process enormous amounts of data, rapidly learn from it, and what's more, apply that knowledge to suggest informed action paths, all at a velocity that can't be matched by humans. This combination cements technology's status in providing groundbreaking potential in the pursuit of transformational change. It points us toward novel paths to change and propels us toward previously unimaginable achievements, and in so doing becomes an inspiring source of personal energy and inspiration for making your own attempts to solve problems big and small, across numerous fields of discovery.

There is no doubt that we are in an era that allows us to connect the immense potential of human ingenuity with the unique qualities of responsible machine learning. DaVinci is a useful example because it allows us to see SustainChain's value as a viable and accessible utility for making major impact, and AI as a common good.

(continued)

(continued)

These capabilities not only hold the power to amplify insights and fast-track actions, but to be an unprecedented source of transparency and accountability, too. In addition, it creates the potential to enhance both our individual and collective ability to shape the future in novel ways, even perhaps to face humanity's biggest tests, like climate change, economic justice, and maybe even world peace.

It is of course incumbent upon us as humans to do whatever we can to ensure that we are using AI ethically and responsibly. That includes recognizing its impact on climate. AI relies on the consumption of enormous amounts of energy, especially fossil fuels—not just in the algorithmic models it powers, but the scale-up of infrastructure and use that is needed if it is to achieve its maximum potential. The consumption of energy by data centers worldwide, which are used to train and run deep learning models behind tools like ChatGPT, has risen dramatically in the last couple of years, constituting an energy footprint that outpaces entire nations (Zewe, 2025). That means raising the energy efficiency of AI is crucial if it is to truly represent a long-term, viable path. A pressing challenge we have is to ensure that AI development can evolve toward being fueled by a combination of renewable energy sources. Concern is warranted as the shift from fossil fuel reliance will have to be tackled swiftly, particularly given how rapidly its use is growing. However, there is also much reason for hope, given AI's unique quality of being its own potential path for discovering ways to address its damage.

All of this will prove essential in pursuing most forms of fundamental change. The climate and sustainability case is but one that illustrates the potential of pairing ethical AI with other advanced technologies and the internet: It shows how, when using these technical capabilities in tandem, they can become *both* a gateway for overcoming the "impossible" *and* a responsible ally as well.

PART IV

Implementing for Impact

With the foundational elements and framework established, the unprecedented power of utilizing the most advanced technologies clear, and the changemaker playbook in hand, this part shifts focus for a final time to take your preparedness to the next level. It covers four additional factors that are needed to achieve the full effect of your new capabilities. The nature of change is revisited to help explain the distinction between the impact of taking action that has always been within you to do, and that which relies on the contributions of many others.

These chapters explore how you can use the playbook to help manifest these contributions and the source of hope it carries if we succeed to create entirely new futures. It also revisits some of the activist weapons discussed in previous parts of the book with a fresh emphasis on their ability to foster human connection, a sense of shared responsibility, and unified action; finally, it explains how the unique characteristics of social media may be a

21st-century solution hiding in plain sight as an elixir for achieving all of these.

- Chapter 7 revisits the concept of connection and the importance of taking actions that closely reflect the interconnected nature of underlying challenges. It explains how the numerous parts of a solution must work together, and the importance of building networks to fill essential gaps in roles, skills, and other needs for implementation.
- Chapter 8 builds on points made regarding connection to expand upon the role of unified action introduced in previous chapters. It illustrates by way of a real example its ability to be a gateway and catalyst for galvanizing people and communities across geographies, and make seemingly impossible tasks feel possible.
- Chapter 9 applies the playbook to show how to spark mass awareness and uses an actual white space solution called CitizenChain to illustrate how technologies for good can be a means by which we motivate a needed and shared sense of responsibility, urgent action, and accountability.
- Chapter 10 steps back from the factors reviewed in prior chapters to make the case for coming to a deep understanding of social media's effect on our thoughts, actions, and behaviors, and suggests strongly that the compulsive and addictive engagement that characterizes our relationship with social media might be turned on its head to instill new behaviors for *good*. It describes the elixir-like quality it can have for helping us to form new habits, like consistent and sustained effort.

7 | Consequential Action Takes Connection

You have now reached the fourth and final stage for completing the change-maker playbook journey! The first six chapters of the book provided you with the official building blocks for developing your own personal playbook. You should also be starting to recognize your personal potential for driving impact, and even for effecting far-reaching change. Going back to the home-building metaphor put forth in Chapter 3, you have now laid the foundation by gaining an appreciation for the nature of change, you've built the frame for the structure by learning the importance and the art of process, and you've installed the power lines by harnessing technology. You're now at a fresh and final phase of this analogy—installing the roof and insulation that reinforce a home's viability and strength. You do that by understanding how the *quality* of your actions ultimately determines whether you succeed and the level of impact you will have.

Why Connection Is So Important

The first area you must account for to deliver the most impact possible may now seem obvious, as it's been an ever-present thread of the book: *connection*. It's important to think about the role that connections play in any actions you decide to take. This is especially true given the many ways the word can be defined and used. For your purposes, connection factors in to change-making as a meaningful relationship or bond.

> *connection,* n.: The meaningful relationship or bond between people, ideas, and/or efforts that fosters collaboration, understanding, and shared purpose.

An entire chapter is being devoted to connection because of the important role it plays in the changemaker's playbook.

Over more than three decades I've learned well that the personal impact you can achieve grows in direct proportion with how well the actions you take fit, hand-in-glove, with the inherent interdependencies of the problem you seek to solve. Let's take a moment to unpack this. The idea of "connection" was introduced in the very first pages of the book and has repeatedly shown up all the way up to this point, where you will now focus on its essential role in creating your *readiness* to act.

Thus far the playbook you've been building is a guide for creating the conditions to tackle changemaking thoughtfully and for avoiding major pitfalls along the way. With a number of examples provided for illustration and reference, you have also observed the importance of the changemaker playbook process, defining the current and future state, and utilizing leading-edge technologies like AI to strengthen your ability to spot gaps and connect the dots between them. Now have a close look at the importance of *connected action* as it is the only way to achieve and accelerate *outcomes*. There is a critical distinction between the two to account for in your approach.

Connections Lead to Outcomes: The Network Effect

Combining rapidly evolving technology with ever-expanding webs of knowledge and people creates a special kind of potential for driving unprecedented levels of impact and change. Specifically, as these webs grow, they uncover vast synergies among and across them through a force known as the *network effect* (see Figure 7.1).

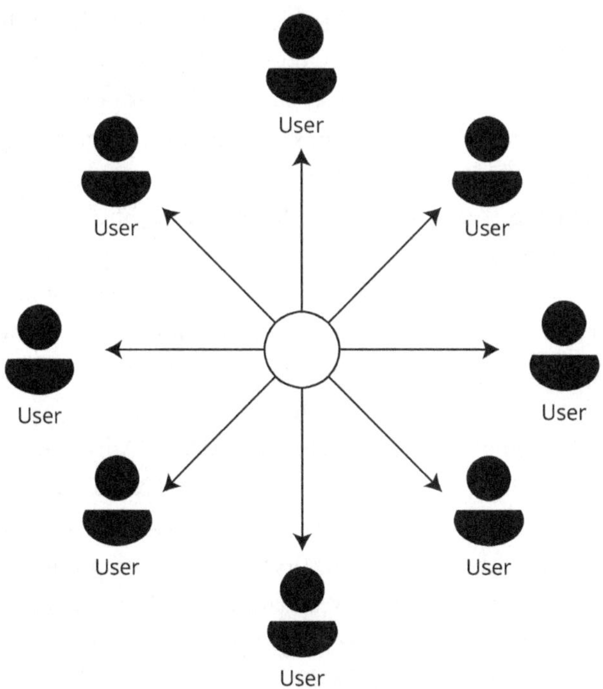

Figure 7.1   The network effect.

> *network effect,* n.: As a social phenomenon; a pattern of interconnected individuals who actively exchange information, resources, and support for personal, professional, or communal benefit.

As you're about to see, the network effect is a phenomenon that adds a whole new dimension to the real, simultaneous, and connected action we can each create. This is chiefly due to the phenomenon's particular nature, wherein the value of a network or system increases *exponentially* with the number of users, connections, and interactions. By understanding how network effects uncover these synergies, we can go on to design and cultivate communities that foster innovation, collaboration, and growth. As more users or components needed to drive progress on a problem are added to the network, the number of potential connections and interactions grows with them. As the network expands, the links among them begin to reveal hidden synergies between what otherwise seem like unrelated elements.

Imagine a network of researchers, scientists, and engineers from diverse fields like AI, biotechnology, and psychology. As they connect, interact, and share their knowledge and expertise, the number of potential connections and interactions they make expands exponentially. Seemingly unrelated concepts and ideas begin to intersect and influence each other. AI algorithms inform the design of more efficient biotechnology processes, and insight from cognitive psychology improves the development of more intuitive AI interfaces. Scientists and engineers can discover new materials, and the diversity and interconnectedness of the researchers allow them to approach complex problems from new angles, leading to innovative solutions.

One such example helped develop the World Wide Web. In the 1980s, a network of researchers, scientists, and engineers came together and connected their work on the internet and hypertext systems, sharing their knowledge, ideas, and expertise. Tim Berners-Lee, who proposed the idea of the World Wide Web, and Robert Cailliau, who collaborated to develop the web's fundamental technology, were both from CERN. Marc Andreessen, who developed the Mosaic web browser that popularized the web, and Eric Bina, who contributed to development of the Mosaic browser, were both from the National Center for Supercomputing Applications (NCSA). Together, they contributed to the creation of a decentralized, collaborative environment, where no single organization or individual is in control. People from various backgrounds, disciplines, and organizations share knowledge and built on one another's work to create something groundbreaking and revolutionary. This is a great example of an invention that without the proper collaboration might not have happened, and where the value and utility continue to increase to this day, as more users and websites are continuously added to the network.

Network effects create feedback loops, where the *output* of one interaction becomes the *input* for another. These loops then amplify and reinforce synergies and can even lead to new properties and behaviors. In the web example, the feedback loops caused the network of users and communities comprising the internet to continuously grow and evolve. We can imagine, for example, that the researchers and scientists at CERN and other institutions began using the web, providing feedback on its functionality and usability. Berners-Lee and his team refined the web's technologies based on user feedback to make it more user-friendly. Then, as more users and developers joined the web, they created new content, applications, and tools, which in turn provided feedback to the web's developers. This feedback loop continued, with each interaction leading to further refinements and improvements in the web's performance, security, and functionality.

As the network grows, it starts to reach critical mass, where the number of interactions and connections within it becomes sufficient to create a self-reinforcing cycle of unlocking new synergies. This dynamic generates still more new ideas and innovations that can ultimately transform the fields involved. Wonderfully, network effects thrive on diversity and complexity; as the network grows, it incorporates an increasingly wide range of perspectives, expertise, and resources, again leading to a richer and more dynamic environment where still more synergies can emerge. Because of their nature, network effects can also create nonlinear behavior, where small changes can have disproportionately large effects.

The hashtag feature first introduced by Twitter in 2007 is a classic example of this. It began when a small group of users started using hashtags to categorize and make their tweets discoverable. As more users joined Twitter and began using hashtags, the feature became increasingly valuable to users, helping to identify and amplify trending topics and providing a whole new way for users to discover and engage with content. The hashtag phenomenon led to other innovative applications, like social activism and community building; those with similar interests could make use of this feature to easily create new communities and networks.

Once you understand how the network effect can uncover (sometimes unpredictable) synergies, you can utilize it to design and cultivate systems that foster groundbreaking innovation, behaviors, and impact. This underscores its usefulness to changemakers looking to achieve actual outcomes.

Connections Lead to Super Networks

You should now place all that power and potential to the side for a moment, because the network effect on its own can't ensure that benefits will be generated from the synergies it reveals. For that to happen, you need the next step: to forge the creation of "super networks." Super networks can also be thought of as *networks-of-networks* (see Figure 7.2).

> *network-of-networks,* or *super network,* n.: A group of interconnected networks, which are themselves a group of interconnected people or things.

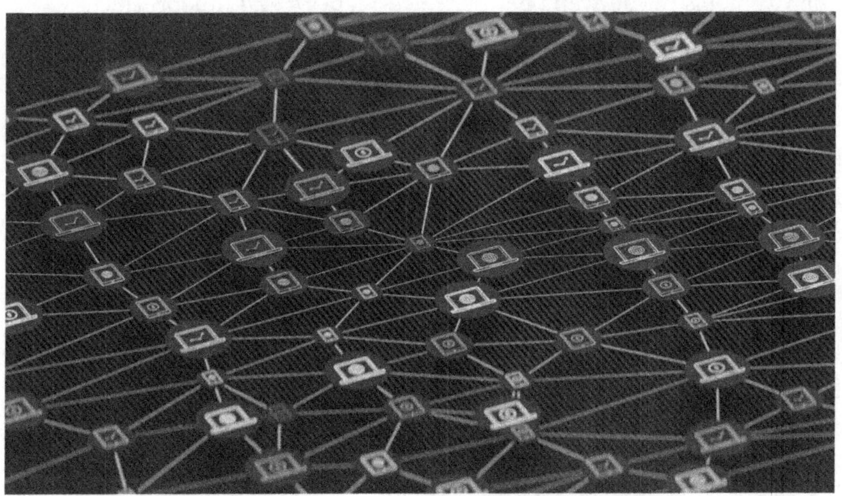

Figure 7.2   Network-of-networks.

In short, a network-of-networks dramatically amplifies—supercharges, if you will—the impact of the network effect, far beyond what any individual, group, or network can achieve on its own.

You can understand the difference between creating a *dynamic network effect* and creating a *super network* by breaking it down a little further. The former enables connections, interactions, and exchanges between users, encouraging them to engage through features and experiences that motivate participation and contribution. A dynamic network effect facilitates interaction that creates a feedback loop, allowing users to build on each other's contributions; in addition, it continually improves the platform or system to create larger behavioral trends, impacts, and outcomes.

A network-of-networks (or super network), by comparison, maximizes the synergies uncovered by connecting and integrating *multiple* networks, systems, or platforms. It combines them to create unified, cohesive ecosystems, ensures seamless communication and data exchange between them, and fosters cross-network synergies through collaboration, innovation, and knowledge sharing. Thus, a super network continuously refines its ability to maximize the benefits of its collective linkage and minimize redundancies. Its potential is therefore proportionate to the exponential growth of behaviors and outcomes taking place because of it.

In short, the network effect focuses on a single system (e.g., a supply chain, geography, or community), while a super network involves integrating an interconnected set of communities made up of multiple networks and systems (e.g., supply chains across industries, geographies, and focus areas). Figure 7.3 shows super networks around the globe.

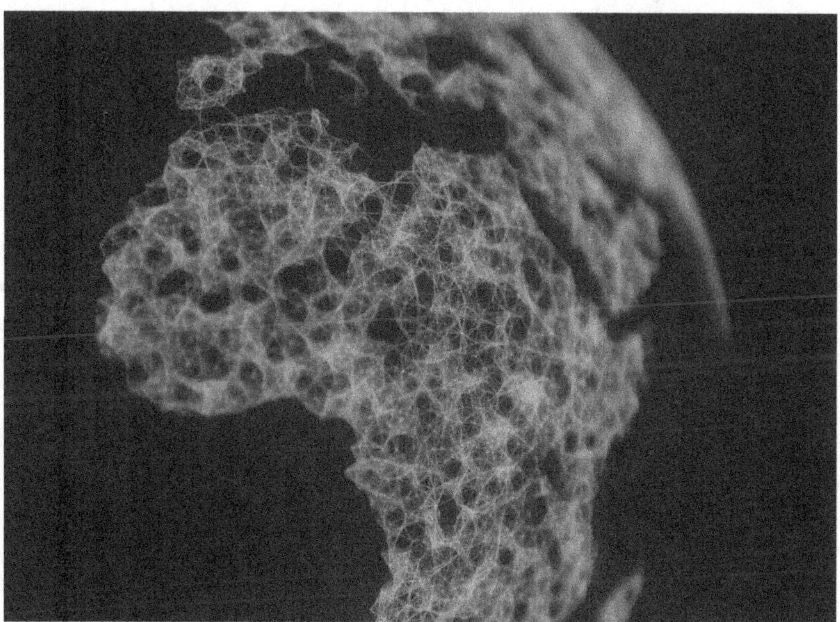

Figure 7.3   Super networks that span the globe!

Network effects maximize their value in a single network or system (like Facebook), while super networks maximize synergies *across* multiple networks and systems (like the internet). As super networks spread and grow, they inherently become capable of a bigger and more complex impact, integrating and standardizing relationships across the many networks and systems that make them up as they expand.

When you think about whether you can have impact in this context, the possibilities begin to feel endless and exciting!

The Network Effect and SustainChain

At any given moment, the staggering number of individual people, projects, innovations, collaborations, investments, studies, solutions, and so on that might surround a big problem—whether or not they are occurring independently of one another or benefit from access to shared intelligence and coordinated action—is nothing short of astounding. By some estimates, the number is in the hundreds of millions. Knowing this, and knowing now the importance of unified action, refer back now to the SustainChain story and reflect on whether you think the network effect is in play.

If you think so, you are correct. Now consider whether SustainChain is a super network. If you think yes, you are again correct. It is. Indeed, it is only because SustainChain is both of these things that it is possible to envision it as a platform for meeting world-scale challenges, like food, water, and energy security. These are, or at the very least are certainly among, the most complex and intertwined sets of issues we currently face as humans. Super networks that represent all the individual parts of the world's *value chains* (another word for supply chain) and their underlying support systems are the *only* way to pull off total resiliency, let alone sustainability, and certainly to do so fast enough. Super networks that incorporate all the individual actions and efforts are also the only way to translate them into consequential action.

Reaching that future—where we have achieved supply chain resiliency—requires building a network-of-networks that can cultivate the greatest number of synergies across networks. It needs to provide a window for viewing a multitude of existing gaps—the missing links in the chain, if you will—and create awareness of the connections that must be made, whether that's a new resource, an innovation, a solution, or a partnership. Weaving together groups of people who bring their unique perspectives, talents, and contributions to the table will be an essential factor for making the biggest changes we need to effect.

Connection and interconnection, then, are the fiber of achieving true transformation. As you break problems down, you can observe their underlying issues, create possible solutions, tailor actions, build blueprints for change, and most importantly, execute on them. Seeing these things is not only *important* to reach the future state, but as you've now seen in a variety of situations, *fundamental*. Doing so makes it possible to account for critical interdependencies (from *top-down* policies, bottom-up social/people considerations, critical investments, etc.) that contribute in consequential ways to good outcomes. Simply put, seeing the connections and accounting for them empowers us to make the possible, possible.

More Ways to Consider the Benefits of Super Networks

Think about this: The Climate Action Network, a global coalition of organizations working to address climate change, has nearly 2,000 member organizations from over 130 countries (Climate Action Network, n.d.). An immense number of initiatives to address climate change from governments, philanthropists, NGOs, and individuals alike are all taking place simultaneously as of the writing of this book. It's certainly wonderful, but it also makes it very difficult to assess what actions will move the needle the most, and will do so more quickly. What's more, these collections of people and practices—just as with the number and array of organizations discussed in Chapter 5 that inspired the creation of SustainChain—are rife with duplicated effort and waste. There are also many efforts that are working at cross purposes with one another and competing for the same funding without realizing that they might be undermining one another's efforts. A lack of awareness of these types of issues is obscuring important opportunities to combine efforts, partner, and collaborate. In short, we are literally working against ourselves!

When links and efforts that might complement one another can be brought to the surface using AI engines like DaVinci, it not only means we have a way to connect them, but we can also set the network effect into full motion and begin to uncover untold synergies that ultimately create paths to whole *new* futures. Using visualization tools like SustainChain's Mission Control adds to this dynamic by allowing us to observe "hot spots" of momentum, inform us of areas that may not yet be receiving enough focus, and raise our awareness of new avenues that prove key to our overall progress.

Being prepared to contribute effectively to a goal that ensures global food security, for instance, will require taking effective action on all major fronts of the entire food supply system—improving soil health, increasing agricultural productivity and sustainable farming practices, supporting small-scale farmers and local food systems, improving food distribution and waste reduction systems, and more. Each of these and other key elements of effecting change at this level are, themselves, connected. Similarly, the actions required to achieve the impact must also be connected.

Figure 7.4 is helpful for reinforcing the point. As with any other global supply chain that supports basic needs, reinforcing its resilience and overall sustainability requires providing access for everyone across the total chain (from the farmers, manufacturers, distributors, and retailers, to resource recovery) to what they need to succeed (funding, innovation, expertise, partners, etc.). When looking at the full picture in this way, it leaves little doubt that having the practical ability to connect the biggest dots is a changemaker's gateway for effecting true systems-based outcomes.

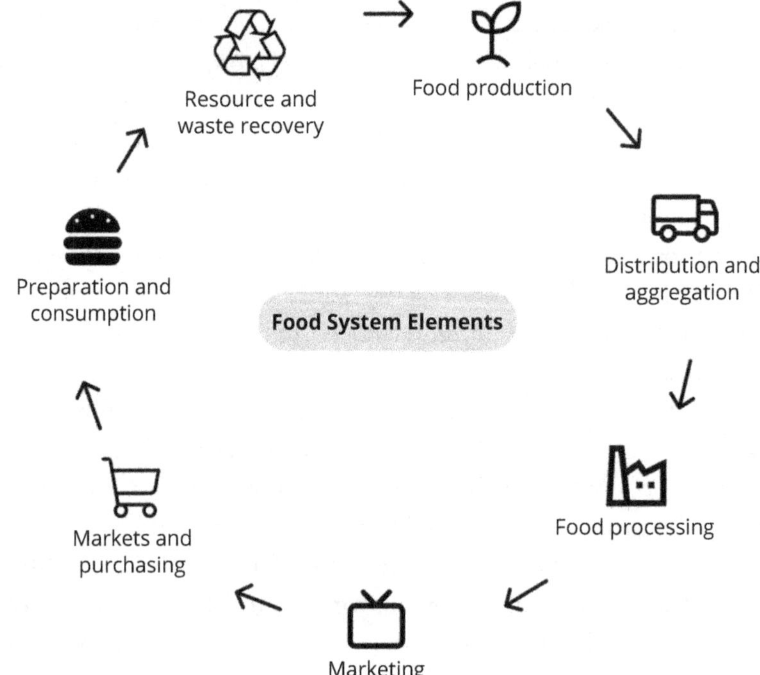

Figure 7.4   Food system value chain.

SustainChain creates this type of access for changemakers across the entire food system supply chain, and contributes directly to establishing these required connections in two key ways:

- First, it provides the possibility for those who *represent* a source of what is needed to effect change to find those who *need* what they're supplying.
- Second, as the network-of-networks that SustainChain represents continues to expand, so does the likelihood that a connection between the two will be made.

In being a product of the very changemaker process embedded within the playbook, SustainChain has a built-in capability to contribute to a changemaker's readiness.

Connect the Pieces

This may seem impossibly complicated but, as with many other points made throughout the book, is more straightforward than it might seem at first glance. Consider it through the lens of SustainChain's very specific role in assisting with efforts to rebuild global supply chains in order to fortify the food system against possible crises and contribute to its overall stability. While highly sophisticated in its design, the tech is a simple utility that is providing a source of automation and intelligence to support broad-based action, make progress possible and easier to organize, and to do these things with hyper *efficiency*.

Just as the web created a tremendous global network of interlinked computers and servers that exchange massive amounts of data and online communication, action networks power the mass mobilization of activity needed to make real progress. The reinforcement learning capability at SustainChain's core creates novel opportunities to advance change because of its ability to find critical paths to action, and even to continually enhance its own capability for doing so, but it's the realm of networks to power the size and potential of those opportunities. A stunningly high number of interconnected actions *can* occur if links like those DaVinci continuously identifies can effectively reach those in the best position to implement them, and even more importantly, only if that implementation *happens*. As you may have guessed, that takes us all the way back to square one of achieving any impact at all. . .the actual *doing*.

Simultaneously rebuilding global supply chains as quickly as possible will most certainly take all the things we know that SustainChain was designed to create: a neutral space and community with visibility into one another's work, and data intelligence (observations generated by DaVinci) to dynamically guide their actions, across different geographies, industries, and so on. However, you might ask (and are certainly correct to do so): Isn't SustainChain's power to potentially create whole new futures ultimately limited by the total number of people and roles that make up its member community at any point in time? And the answer to that question is, indisputably, *yes*! It is precisely where the critical role of action networks enters the scene. Even more important than the connections themselves are the synchronicity and speed of the actions.

I discuss this further in the next chapter; be on the lookout for this key concept to come up again.

Key Takeaways

Your initial encounter with connection as a critical element of changemaking was in the first chapter of the book, where I shared the importance of striking a necessary balance between individual *me* action and collective *we* action. That chapter discussed the success factors that drove the ultimate eradication of polio, specifically referencing the combination of research, advocacy, and other types of effort that were needed—including the massive orchestration of the thousands of people who carried out the vaccination campaigns—in order to achieve the ultimate 99 percent decrease in polio cases worldwide. You saw that overcoming the polio epidemic didn't *end* with Jonas Salk's discovery of the vaccine, but in actuality *began* with it. It was achieving the connection across what must have felt like an impossible number of interrelated dots—groups of people, skills, scientists, and funding—that made it possible to accomplish this life-saving outcome.

Without a doubt, the same will be true if we are successful at securing a sustainable supply of food, water, and energy as we travel into the future. The polio vaccine's success established the point that world-scale impact is achieved through (1) attacking numerous interrelated parts in a well-orchestrated way, (2) combining our individual achievements with networks of accomplishment, and (3) persisting on steps 1 and 2 with a mindset that naturally accounts for critical connections and continued adjustment.

In Chapter 5, I used the SustainChain example to show how applying the changemaker playbook process can result in creating a platform dedicated to forging essential partnerships across efforts, connecting changemakers to the right tools, skillsets, and partnerships. You left the chapter observing how SustainChain as a platform, in tandem with its DaVinci AI engine and Mission Control visualization tool, became a technology trio purpose-built to accommodate the connected nature of big change, both within and outside business. It gave you a way to understand how you equip yourself to manage stratospheric complexity and to do so in a way that allows you to stay focused on your own unique piece of the puzzle, while the machine continuously learns from your actions and shares the lessons across the community.

Chapter 2 was used to help you step back from the big picture and demonstrate how breaking down a problem consistently and naturally sheds light on the underlying issues and the nature of the actions needed to succeed. I did so in part by highlighting the pattern to changemaking that I've personally experienced over many years of engaging in large corporate settings, and sharing the common trait of successful efforts to improve intertwined systems. I also reviewed the steps used to identify issues that businesses and products might share and the importance of building an end-to-end understanding of them.

(continued)

(continued)

From all of these parts of your journey thus far, you now know:

- Changemakers can take actions that have the potential to achieve meaningful impact, and sometimes even to fully overcome complex challenges, if they commit to uncovering the most significant underlying issues and their inherent connections.
- Changemakers can reveal these connections if they engage in a structured yet flexible process.
- If they are disciplined in the steps they take and observing their effects, this will lead to appreciating the systems-based nature of effecting change, and they'll get better at distinguishing the current state from the future state, while adjusting accordingly.
- Finally, changemakers must adopt a mindset that accounts for each of these steps and plan and act accordingly.

What are the chances for success? Personal impact that contributes to transformational change is success by definition. Any action that lifts the possibilities or accelerates needed change *is* consequential action. In the specific case of SustainChain, DaVinci can create profound opportunities that previously did not exist on their own, or even continually enhance its own capability to do so, but it's the actions taken across the super network of SustainChain users that powers the collective potential to ensure water, food, and energy security.

SustainChain ended up being both a tool for tackling fragmented efforts to combat climate change, and a solution in itself—but the critical takeaway from this chapter is actually a caveat:

SustainChain alone is not enough to solve the problem of supply chain resilience.

The key factor is still the connected actions of all its users, unified in purpose. SustainChain was specifically designed with this in mind, bringing order and connection to building resilient new supply chains through an ever-expanding community of changemakers. It may go without saying, but AI is simply a device for attacking problems in a systems-oriented way—it is up to all involved to use this device in a way that advances their goals.

Every time DaVinci identifies a suggested action that is not yet taking place, SustainChain picks up that baton and continually nudges relevant members of the community to act with greater urgency. Using digital prompts (informed by the preferences selected by each user), DaVinci is constantly reminding users of the possible impact of their actions they can take to close the gap (provide the missing link in the chain, as it were).

Thus, a stunningly high number of interconnected actions *can* occur if the connections DaVinci continuously identifies effectively reach those who can best implement them, and that implementation happens. As you might have guessed, that takes us all the way back to the single most consequential piece of the personal impact puzzle. . .the actual *doing*.

To conclude, connection represents our shared journey toward swift action and transformation, and an affirmation of our shared human spirit. As interwoven networks of people and data grow, the network effect begins to speed things up exponentially and, in turn, dramatically amplify the impact of our actions far beyond what any individual, group, or single network can achieve without it.

Is this now everything we need to know and all we need to do? Yes. . .but also, no.

8

Together: The Power and Promise of Unified Action

As you will no doubt now agree, taking action is the ultimate means for achieving any end. That said, not all actions are created equal, and establishing the linkages needed for driving the personal impact you're after isn't adequate on its own. You've now seen that digital technology literally connects us, and that AI deepens our understanding while uncovering new paths to travel. You also learned in the last chapter about the ability of super networks (or networks-of-networks) to tap into our collective energy and foster connection. Each of these plays an essential part in driving the greatest possible impact through your actions. However, *unified* action is the enabler for effecting the biggest change possible.

SustainChain and its learning engine provide an enormous source of support for taking such actions. If we take full advantage of its technical capabilities and allow AI engines like DaVinci to guide our actions, we will most certainly make progress. But the extent of the impact you can bring about in this way is greatest when you can also fully apply the capabilities of these technologies toward fostering unified action. Put another way, your ability to create change is at times determined by how much we engage in action *together and concurrently*: Collective and simultaneous effort is the only true path to world-scale outcomes.

It is through this lens that you can observe why actions are not created equal. While every intention to bring about meaningful ethical change deserves appreciation and all actions taken in its pursuit our respect, those we undertake in concert with others who share our goals will naturally lead to greater impact—and increasingly so, as the complexity and scale of a problem grows.

A powerful illustration of this effect can be seen in a personal experience that I was privileged to contribute to on the African continent, which I share with you now to make the lesson more real.

The Millennium Villages Project

Other than world peace and climate change, ending extreme poverty may be the world's biggest and most complicated problem to be solved. The number of individuals and organizations contributing their time, resources, and funds to address it and/or foster economic justice is too dispersed to quantify. And while no single figure can capture the full extent of these efforts, even a cursory look at available data shows that hundreds of millions of individuals worldwide are actively engaged in efforts to address extreme poverty, through donations, volunteering, organizing, and so on. In the United States alone, for example, 15 percent of people support hunger and homelessness causes, and nearly a third of all Americans formally volunteer at least once a year (TeamStage, 2022). Thousands of organizations and coalitions exist globally, working to alleviate the effects of poverty (Borgen, 2018). To some extent, these efforts have paid off; the number of people living in poverty globally has steadily declined since 1990 (World Bank, 2024).

However, the same data that shows that poverty has declined significantly in the last several decades also demonstrates that global poverty reduction has come to a "near standstill" (World Bank, 2024). Approximately 700 million people worldwide continue to suffer from extreme poverty, defined as living on less than $2.15 per day. This is about 8.5 percent of the global population. The majority of those living in extreme poverty are concentrated in sub-Saharan Africa and South Asia, with sub-Saharan Africa accounting for about two-thirds of the world's extreme poor. In addition, the number of people living on less than $6.85 per day has remained about the same for the past three and a half decades. Senior World Bank leadership has stressed that the "feeble" pace of alleviating world poverty is insufficient to address the problem within the next century, warning that a "business-as-usual approach will no longer work" (World Bank Group, 2024). Indeed, much of the progress gained in recent history has been stalled or even reversed by such factors as the COVID-19 pandemic, slow economic growth, high debt, and geopolitical conflict, among others.

Intuitively or otherwise, we sense the inherent complexities of the problem—culture, history, politics, and physical geographic considerations are among the largest contributors. These are all part of a broader web of interconnected root causes and structural barriers. So why point to this area to reinforce the central message of this chapter that working together is the most crucial part of effecting widespread change? The story I'm about to share will help shine a very bright light on this point.

In 2005, there was an extraordinary and courageous attempt by one of the foremost macroeconomists in the world, Professor Jeffrey Sachs, to implement a wide-reaching economic development program to address extreme poverty's root causes on a global scale. This was aimed at combating what he refers to in his lauded book *The End of Poverty* as the *poverty trap* (see Figure 8.1).

poverty trap, n.: A self-reinforcing cycle where extremely poor individuals or countries lack sufficient capital—such as human, business, infrastructure, natural, institutional, and knowledge capital—to make productive investments and escape poverty.

According to his economic expertise, Professor Sachs suggested that the poverty trap could be eliminated by providing a holistic, integrated package of interventions—covering agriculture, health, education, infrastructure, and business development—to meet basic needs in poor rural communities. To that end, he architected a comprehensive, systems-based approach that put integrated economic development at the center of a 15-year effort. The model aimed to create a "critical platform" of essential services and

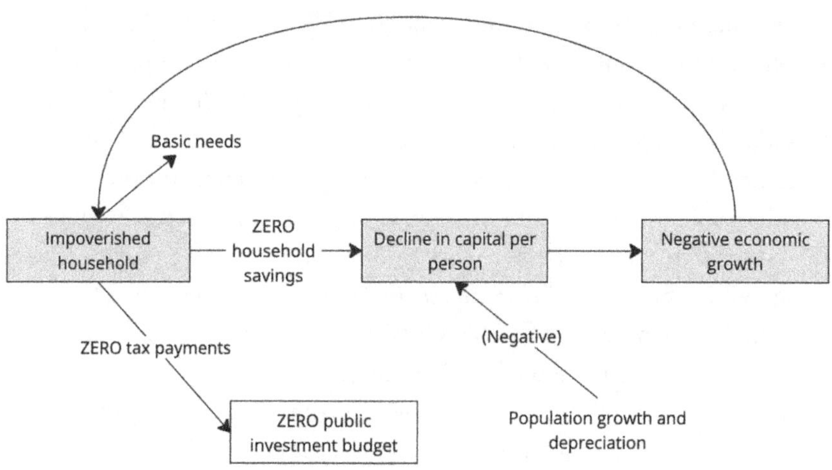

Figure 8.1   The poverty trap.

Source: Sachs (2005).

investments, enabling communities to generate income, improve health, and achieve sustainable growth. And the overarching approach used to implement that model aligned strongly with the framework embedded within this playbook! Indeed, as you'll see, many of the dynamics discussed throughout this book are clearly visible in the project's design.

Known as the *Millennium Villages Project (MVP),* it was specifically aimed at ending extreme poverty in sub-Saharan Africa. Grounded in the belief that poverty is not the result of laziness or fate, but rather structural and environmental traps, the approach reflected a deliberate attempt to bridge global development goals with local realities.

The MVP was structured as a proof-of-concept: Rather than a massive policy initiative, it focused on a dozen or so pilot villages across multiple countries, each selected to be broadly representative of rural Africa. The project's architecture reflected a deliberate attempt to bridge top-down economic development goals with the practical realities of life in the village community. Figure 8.2 shows the site map outlining these pilot villages.

Professor Sachs understood very deeply the realities surrounding poverty: namely, that it is not the result of any single factor, and therefore cannot be addressed in isolation. Instead, the MVP model implemented integrated programs across multiple sectors, all critical to successfully transition

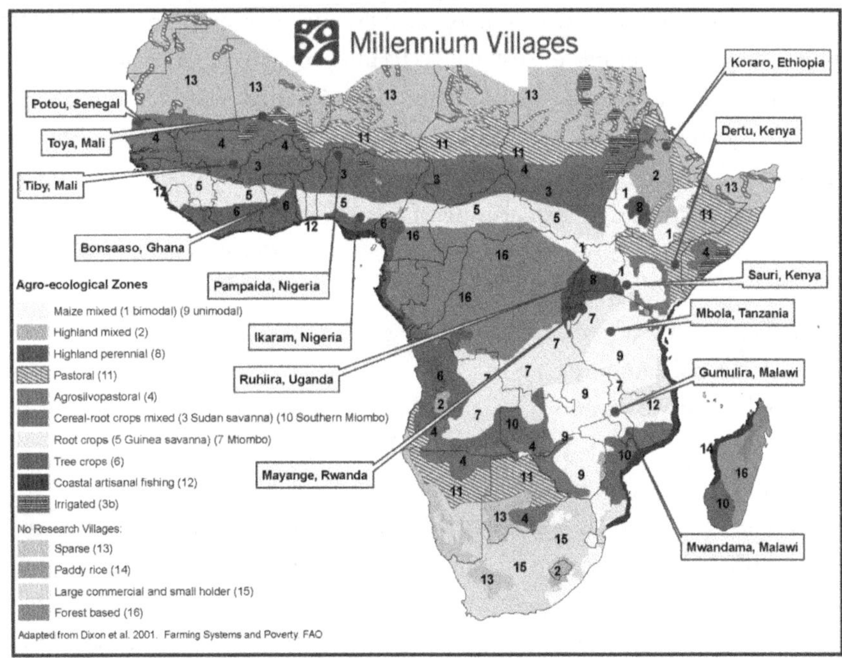

Figure 8.2   Millennium Villages site map.

communities out of extreme poverty—agriculture, health, education, infrastructure, and economic development—simultaneously. By addressing these sectors concurrently, the MVP aimed to create a "virtuous cycle," where improvements in one area reinforced gains in others. Improved crop yields were not enough without access to clean water; education was ineffective without adequate nutrition; and economic growth was unsustainable without basic healthcare. The MVP's model emphasized the interconnected nature of these areas as well as the synergies between them, exemplifying one of the main tenets of the playbook—that only through *coordinated* measures could communities escape the poverty trap.

One of the project's most innovative features was its top-down and bottom-up design. Sachs and his team provided scientific expertise, funding, and coordination (top-down), while local communities were engaged in identifying priorities and implementing solutions (bottom-up). Village leaders, teachers, farmers, and health workers were included in decision-making processes, ensuring that interventions were relevant, culturally appropriate, and locally supported. For example, agricultural input subsidies were introduced alongside training in sustainable farming practices, while local clinics were stocked with malaria bed nets and essential medicines, often administered by community health workers trained through the program. Just like the playbook you've been building, this blend of expert-driven strategy and grassroots participation was a cornerstone of the MVP's philosophy.

The MVP specifically targeted interconnected development challenges:

- Food security was addressed through improved seeds, fertilizer access, and farmer training.
- Clean water came via boreholes, wells, and sanitation programs.
- Education was supported by building schools, supplying materials, and providing school meals.
- Health initiatives included malaria prevention, maternal care, and HIV/AIDS treatment.

These were not isolated efforts, but rather interdependent parts of a single developmental ecosystem. The underlying theory was that simultaneous progress in each area would create a self-reinforcing cycle of growth and resilience, leading to lasting change.

As an experiment in development economics, the MVP made a profound contribution to the global pursuit of economic justice. It challenged the fatalism that often surrounds poverty and provided empirical evidence that, with the right kind of investment, even the world's poorest communities could build sustainable pathways to prosperity. Importantly, it helped shift the narrative from "aid versus no aid" to a more nuanced discussion about how aid should be structured and delivered. The MVP's work was also groundbreaking in helping to localize and test global commitments in real-world settings. By demonstrating how systemic change could occur at the village level, it inspired similar approaches and informed subsequent global development strategies.

Despite its ambitions and successes, the project naturally encountered several obstacles to success. Similar to some of the other examples discussed (BrightLine's pivot, for instance), several critical adjustments were made to benefit from the incredible learnings being generated along the way. This, again, returns to another key attribute of a winning playbook that I've pointed to several times: that approaching change efforts with *flexibility* and *adaptability* to evolving circumstances is an essential part of effective change-making. For example, political instability, logistical hurdles, and local governance challenges complicated implementation in some villages. Nevertheless, the MVP remains a landmark initiative in developmental thinking—one that emphasized *integration* over *fragmentation* and demonstrated that poverty, when attacked from all angles and with sustained effort, can indeed be overcome.

By achieving milestones like those shown in Figure 8.3, the MVP provided a replicable blueprint challenging the notion that poverty in Africa is intractable. Its emphasis on data-driven adaptation and partnerships with

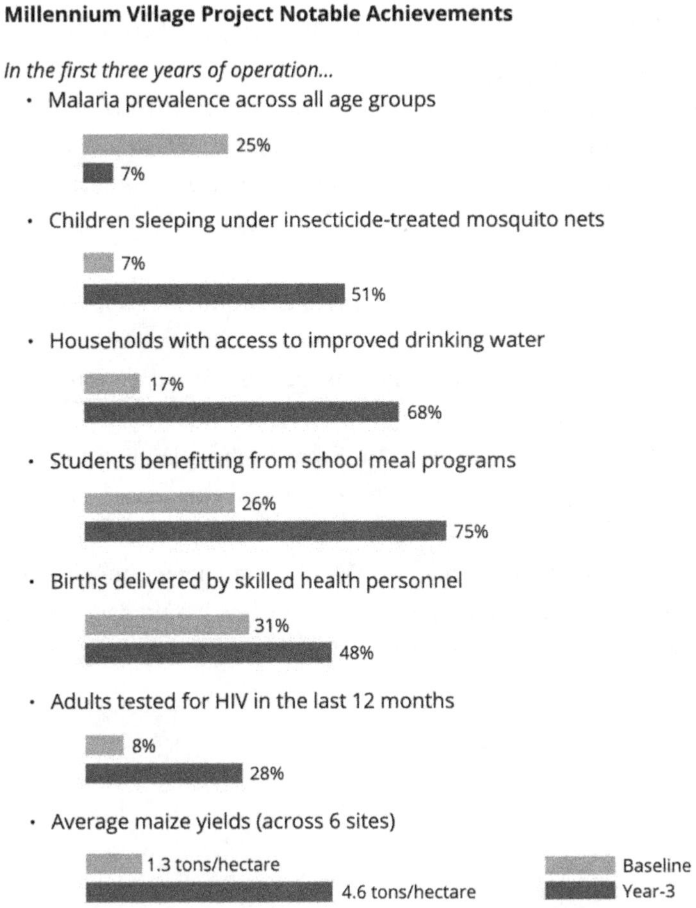

Millennium Village Project Notable Achievements

In the first three years of operation...
- Malaria prevalence across all age groups

  25%

  7%

- Children sleeping under insecticide-treated mosquito nets

  7%

  51%

- Households with access to improved drinking water

  17%

  68%

- Students benefitting from school meal programs

  26%

  75%

- Births delivered by skilled health personnel

  31%

  48%

- Adults tested for HIV in the last 12 months

  8%

  28%

- Average maize yields (across 6 sites)

  1.3 tons/hectare

  4.6 tons/hectare

  Baseline

  Year-3

Figure 8.3   Millennium Village project achievements, 2005–2010.
Source: Shaw (2011).

African institutions also helped shift development paradigms from charity to *collaborative problem-solving*. It advanced global understanding of poverty alleviation by testing integrated development at scale. Its successes in specific sectors highlighted the potential of holistic approaches, while its shortcomings underscored the complexity of sustaining progress in resource-constrained environments without sustained and adequate funding. By blending scientific rigor with community participation, the project left a legacy of lessons on balancing ambition with feasibility in the pursuit of economic justice.

You may be wondering how I know these things, or where my insight into the MVP's close resemblance to the changemaker's playbook comes from. I had the privilege to be deeply involved in the project. The alignment of my personal playbook for effecting transformational change with Professor Sachs's extraordinary thinking and leadership was a seminal opportunity for me to validate my own practice in a global context: the importance of unified action and the magnitude of impact that can come from it.

Ultimately the MVP was an *integrated* economic development program, wherein all its key sectors were approached simultaneously. In addition, the sectors themselves had important linkages and interrelationships among them—it was futile to look at or act on any individual aspect in pure isolation. And the implementations of Professor Sachs's plan had to reflect these characteristics; top-down groups needed to be formed at the policy and financing level, and the same had to be done bottom-up within and across village communities and across 12 African countries, connecting the work of science teams and other experts. None of this would have been accomplished without unified action within the numerous teams that surrounded the project, and across them.

Key Takeaways

Some have asked the question of whether the MVP worked. I would say that whatever its shortcomings, it remains the finest illustration one could ask for to understand the power of the playbook. This is not because it succeeded in eliminating extreme poverty, but because of what was possible to prove by utilizing unified action and a holistic, multidisciplinary approach. This instance of unified action catalyzed people and communities across geographies and meaningfully addressed all the major aspects of extreme poverty—including education, health, safe water, food security, and many others—generating enormous impact and crucial insights to leverage by the changemakers who follow.

The key takeaway from this chapter is that unified action represents a critical gateway for tackling the world's most pressing problems that sits alongside the fundamental building blocks explored so far—in particular, how numerous pieces of the puzzle must work together (systems), and by extension, how the actions we take can impact one another. In addition, by combining technological innovation with community governance, the MVP provided scalable models for rural development and revealed the unique needs of world-scale economic development and the longer-term financing mechanisms they require.

9

Acid Test for Success: Social Responsibility and Shared Duty

You now have a way to understand—from previous chapters as well as your growing intuition—how critical elements like connection, collaboration, and concerted effort are to generating the impact you are looking to achieve. In this chapter you will learn to account for the final challenge I cover with you: how to bring about the necessary *amount* of action you will need to solve the problem at hand. To be sure, big-picture transformational outcomes like water security require a tremendous amount of effort, motivated by an equally tremendous amount of shared sense of urgency and response. Most wonder if it's even possible to inspire, motivate, and catalyze the level of mass awareness and involvement that world change requires. While this is certainly a good and valid question, the more productive one for a change-maker is to ask *how* we can use the playbook you've been building to get into the strongest position possible to do so, and that is the focus of this penultimate chapter of the book.

Applying the Changemaker Playbook Process

It becomes more and more apparent each day that the changing climate is one of the most time-sensitive issues we face. The urgency, complexity, and magnitude of the issue are a perfect storm, with sweeping implications for the world, and requiring an amount of global unified action we've not yet seen. Because this is so, it is also an important opportunity to explore the robustness of the changemaker framework. You have now observed through a variety of examples that solving problems of any magnitude requires an effort to understand what fundamentally causes and drives them. You will now observe how to draw upon all the insights you've been collecting so far, apply the playbook, engage in the structured thought process shared, and observe the actions that flow from these steps to create consequential world-scale impact!

Step 1: Defining the Issue and Goal

Issue: While many individuals and communities recognize the serious, increasing effects of climate change on people and planet, awareness is neither adequate nor robust enough to create a grassroots movement capable of driving lasting large-scale policy and behavioral change.

Goal: Mobilize sufficient collective action needed at the citizen level to manage the growing effects of climate change on our lives and those of future generations.

Step 2: Comparing the Current and Future State

There are many ways to characterize the current state of civil society's focus on the issue of climate change. However, some of the major ones include the following:

- There is massive worldwide interest: "climate change is on the minds of people everywhere and the results statistically represent 87 percent of the world's population" (UNDP, 2024).
- It's extremely challenging to figure out how and where to find the right opportunities to contribute our actions.
- The collection of total actions being taken are currently insufficient, fragmented, disparate, and uncoordinated.

- We lack visibility or understanding of one another's efforts that could facilitate or support our own.
- We are insufficiently organized, both individually and across organizations.
- We are not clear if or how our actions influence the problems we hope to affect, and/or feel our individual efforts are too small to make a difference (this is referred to as the "tragedy of the commons").
- Given these and other factors, including social, political, and psychological issues, we are challenged to foster sustained passion and activism.

Clearly this is a formidable set of complex challenges to navigate and tackle, and because you know that the gap between the current level of collective action and the magnitude needed from civil society is not the result of any single factor, neither can any of them be addressed in isolation. Once again, we find ourselves at a familiar crossroads: How can you have personal impact and meaningfully contribute to the fundamental change needed in a situation with endless complexities?

Review what's in the toolbox to remind yourself. First and foremost, the changemaker playbook process provides structure for your actions and a way to stay focused; you have the versatility and facility that comes from tapping the most modern forms of technology (the banking examples, SustainChain, DaVinci, and BrightLine are illustrations of the variety of ways this comes into play); and you have the holistic mindset that's been reinforced time and time again throughout these pages. In other words, you are well armed. As long as you act, have the will to stick with it, and adjust your path along the way, success is more than doable.

So let's get back to applying the process, and turn now to defining the *future state:* What does our collective action picture look like if we have solved the current state challenges?

As explored previously—and as is particularly true on this topic—the future state can often fairly easily be defined using a simple inverse of the major challenges describing the current state. Approaching it in this way will obviously not generate an all-inclusive depiction of the future. However, it does something perhaps even more important: It provides a basis for continuing to apply the playbook by keeping you from becoming overwhelmed by both the obvious complexities and the limitless possibilities.

Among other things that could surely be listed, there is little doubt that a robust framework and set of solutions will absolutely be required to address these underlying challenges. To do so, it needs to be able to provide the following:

- Visibility of and access to the individuals, groups, and activities that match our particular climate concerns and areas of passion
- Platforms and tools that allow each of us and our actions to become a seamless part of larger groups and associations dedicated to our goals
- Sources that foster continuous learning, awareness, and developments
- Capabilities that can effectively align and connect the snarl of disparate, fragmented actions currently taking place
- Tools and activities for building and maintaining inspiration, urgency, and focus in our efforts

Ways to address feelings that run counter to what we know to be true, and make people feel that our individual actions *can* have an impact.

Step 3: Performing a Gap Analysis

Assessing the differences between how we characterize the current state and how it would specifically need to change to achieve the future state is the next step in this process. You can round out your thoughts from the current versus future state construct by doing what you did in all previous examples to identify what's missing. First, reflect on the differences between the two, and second, ask *why*:

- Why are organization, alignment, and visibility such difficult challenges to overcome?
- Why has applying the types of tools and platforms used to integrate complex systems in other areas (say, business and research) not worked with climate efforts? In particular, why has it failed to provide a

cohesive source of information that feeds our awareness and understanding of climate-related issues and the actions we can take to help overcome them?

- Why aren't we able to learn from each other more easily? Why are we unable to mobilize effectively and more urgently?

Just like past examples, asking *why* is what allows you to spot issues that lie at the root of the problem and to uncover disconnects that exist between what's needed and the way things are currently designed. You might now ask, isn't it too soon to move to the next step of "setting the plan"? For perfect and complete solutions to these challenges the answer is "yes." But as a basis for making a meaningful contribution with consequential impact, *no,* not at all. Let me show you why.

At this stage in the process, as before, put aside any misgivings on the adequacy of our potential solution and take out our clean sheet of paper to begin imagining how to reach the future state. When you do so, you may find that it engages your thoughts and creativity in such a way that reveals not only an exciting new path to try, but also a white space solution. In this case, the product of our application of the changemaker process is both, in addition to being a direct and exciting extension of SustainChain.

Creating CitizenChain

As explored through the Millennium Villages Project example in the previous chapter, working together and in parallel becomes the most crucial part of effecting widespread change. You also now know that the path to a full transformation of the current to the future state begins with an approach and framework that accounts for the major moving parts and their interrelatedness, as well as a solid commitment to continuous refinement. The same will most certainly hold true for achieving the level of sustained awareness and magnitude of collective citizen action needed to address the effects that the changing climate is having on our lives.

To make the parallel nature of these challenges even clearer, let's review some key similarities in the current state of the citizen action scenario with those that inspired the creation of SustainChain.

You'll recall that the current state in that example pertained to the need to fortify global supply chains from the growing impacts of climate change, and it revealed that an inordinate number of promising actions were already taking place, across organizations of various types and sizes. It was also similarly true that all the good work underway, while substantial, was extremely fragmented, disconnected, and disorganized. Those engaged in both civic action and actions to sustainably rebuild supply chains also shared the common challenge of a general lack of *visibility* to one another's efforts, opportunities for partnership, and access to needed tools, resources, and expertise. There is also the need for changemakers to gain insight and guidance to maximize individual and collective impact as quickly as possible.

SustainChain was the platform solution that emerged from the playbook process to help organizations navigate the tangled mass of actions and sustainably rebuild industrial supply chains with better and faster progress. The data intelligence designed at the very center creates opportunities for continuous, real-time learning from the broader community's actions, and then instantly converts that insight into relevant suggested actions to other community members—all this while providing the needed visibility across its members to foster the crucial collaboration in various areas of focus, like water security and agriculture, simultaneously.

Perhaps given many of the fundamental challenges that SustainChain is built to address and its data intelligent design, it is now clear to see why it can also serve as a strong foundation for the clean sheet of paper design for world-scale citizen awareness and mobilization.

Civic duty and citizen action are the bottom-up piece of achieving climate resilience and overall sustainability. I began to sketch with this part of our changemaker framework in mind, a solution to the major challenges we face in achieving personal impact on climate knowing that it had to check many of the same boxes that SustainChain does. As I reflected, a solution emerged that built on the very same clean sheet as an extension of SustainChain, shaping the technologies used to create capabilities that provide the same usefulness to grassroots, bottom-up, citizen efforts as SustainChain does for organizations. This platform, called *CitizenChain*, was invented to empower and inspire people to pursue their desire to be part of addressing the growing impacts of climate change, as well as support those who are similarly making climate change a priority through their personal action. It was also designed to make inviting others to join in as simple as possible. Let's have a closer look at this outgrowth of the platform using the clean sheet process.

Like SustainChain, AI is generating actionable opportunities and encouraging members to connect, collaborate, and partner on their common links in CitizenChain. As with the SustainChain example, we can use the technology to create a path to success and enable individuals to influence the decisions and actions that organizations prioritize—for-profit, nonprofit, governmental, or otherwise. Figure 9.1 shows the CitizenChain signup screen.

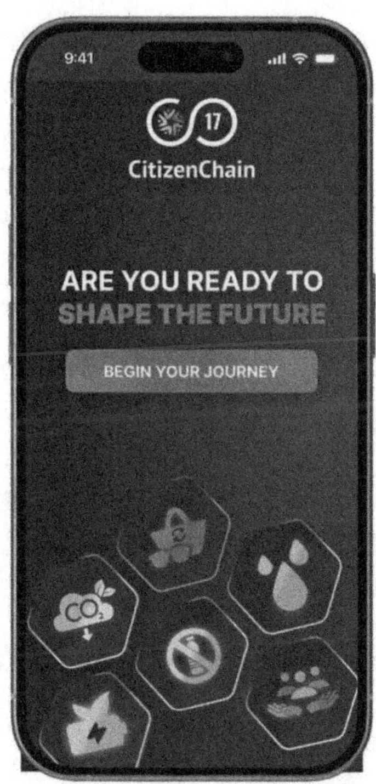

Figure 9.1   CitizenChain signup screen.

Source: With Permission of Paul Allen.

Upon signing up, the platform asks you to identify issues that you'd like to help address, by selecting one or more of the following:

- Plastic Reduction
- Social Equity
- Green Energy Use
- Sustainable Fashion
- Safe Food & Water
- Carbon Reduction

CitizenChain then uses its built-in technological capabilities to provide ways to personally support businesses and other organizations that prioritize the issues you care most about, such as the following:

- The environmental and social impacts of the products and services we consume, and how to make more informed choices
- Ways to motivate and/or agitate by directly sharing our concerns with businesses and urging them to take action
- Encouragement of businesses that are taking tangible steps toward sustainability and urging them to make even faster progress where they can
- Sharing sustainability actions, concerns, and learnings from CitizenChain with social networks to inspire others to join in advocating for change

Similarly, the platform supports the efforts needed to advocate for sustainable policies and help build momentum to catalyze changes at the government level:

- Participate in public campaigns, forums, and town hall meetings to press for policies that align with local needs and priorities
- Take on grassroots actions such as community-based projects, clean-up efforts, and educational programs

Just like SustainChain, the CitizenChain platform is specifically designed to provide opportunities to venture productively down these paths for various types of organizations. In addition, taking actions in this transparent and open environment enabled by advanced technology allows us to engage effectively with one another and help hold each other accountable, while also providing a place for us to contribute our particular talents, expertise, and other actions as a form of public service and civic duty.

Ultimately, a platform like CitizenChain—or so goes the hypothesis embedded in the clean sheet design—can help feed the hope that our individual efforts matter. Since we know that people are often motivated to do something about the climate crisis but either don't necessarily have the means or don't think of themselves as activists, this allows them to find ways to contribute to areas that particularly interest them, as well as find others who share their concerns.

Two other aspects of our citizen action clean sheet design represent capabilities totally unique to CitizenChain. One is that the platform is what's called a *single point aggregator* of opportunities for users to participate and or engage with. Let's consider this a little more deeply:

> *single point aggregator,* n.: A single platform that allows for access to a variety of offerings through one central connection. Instead of dealing with many different providers, you just use the aggregator to reach everything you need in one place.

Part of the challenge identified in our current state scenario when we get inspired to take personal action is not knowing where to begin and how to continue to expand our engagement and progress on our journey toward personal impact. To account for this practical reality in the clean sheet design of CitizenChain, we apply AI to provide that single point access in the different areas we might like to contribute. Here are some examples of the different activity options that allow us to deepen and increase our involvement:

- Educate and raise awareness
- Join or support local organizations
- Advocate for policy change
- Reduce personal carbon footprints
- Support sustainable businesses
- Participate in community projects

- Connect with NGOs and purpose-driven organizations
- Use social media for advocacy
- Connect with global movements

CitizenChain is designed to aggregate opportunities by the different types of actions we may want to take and to venture productively down the paths we select. In so doing, it also accomplishes something else that might be familiar: As all of us continue to use the platform and access opportunities in this way, we build a vast and growing web of connected actions together—a super network (or network-of-networks).

Finally, there's one other unique quality to our clean sheet citizen action design: CitizenChain is *gameified*.

> *gameified*, n.: An activity, process, or system made more engaging by adding elements typical of games, like points, levels, badges, or rewards to motivate participation and enjoyment.

A gameified experience was selected as a strategy for bringing users to the platform in a way that's fun and motivates them to take more and more action. Here's how it works.

First, CitizenChain uses AI to provide opportunities that match the user's selected areas, creating a live, ever-growing set of local, community-based climate and sustainability actions that feed the desire to become active citizens (see Figure 9.2).

Each member user of CitizenChain completes tasks in their chosen impact area to reach new levels of digital activism. They progress by completing the tasks, gaining rewards, and increasing their own education. In doing so, they contribute to the growth of a grassroots movement.

Players can also develop knowledge or skills that apply to real-world problems or settings, such as leadership skills or knowledge of ocean pollution and its specific effects on wildlife. They can also make discoveries on relevant, real-world issues, and even contribute to ongoing problem-solving efforts by supporting experts in the field (see Figure 9.3).

Other educational uses include deeper learning on more niche topics, such as the complexities of city planning. The user can learn more about the realities of this field by planning a virtual city or serve as a vital resource for public input on an issue that city planning experts are presently trying to tackle.

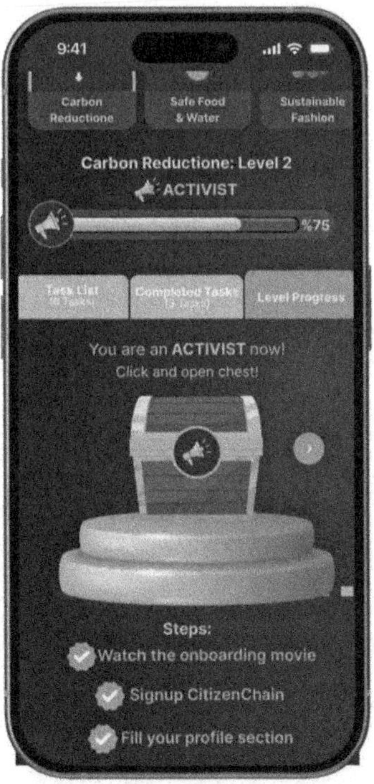

Figure 9.2   CitizenChain action interface.

Source: With Permission of the author.

CitizenChain is designed in this way to bring a fun sense of competition and reward that also satisfies our desire and passion to contribute in practical ways and inspires us to invite our respective networks to expand the chain. It showcases causes that users are most passionate about, connects them with local community members to organize grassroots initiatives, and introduces them to new changemakers and potential mentors interested in similar topics. Users can leverage an interactive and fun environment to learn more about topics or scenarios that are of immediate relevance to the real world and even contribute to ongoing problem-solving efforts by experts in the field, as well as discover new areas of research and innovation, brands or products, initiatives, and organizations to support. And finally, there is the ability to compete with friends and other players within your region, community, or impact area to deepen those connections.

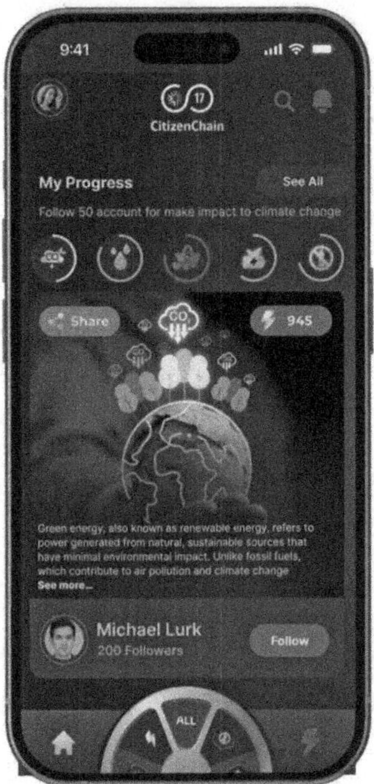

Figure 9.3　CitizenChain progress overview.

Curated facts, figures, and insights (called *breadcrumbs*) are provided for each of the selected impact areas. They inspire users to dig deeper into their impact journeys and take more action. These facts and figures allow players to delve deeper and deeper into their passion areas at every level to keep growing their Personal Impact Quotient. As part of feeding this dynamic, experts can contribute to the breadcrumbs curated as a way to showcase their work in a fun, digestible way (see Figure 9.4).

To summarize, the gamified experiences are simply a way to bring users to the platform that feeds their internal activist 24/7. It provides users with an opportunity to feel that their individual efforts actually matter. For those who don't necessarily have the means or think of ourselves as activists, this allows them to find things that interest them and engage with others who share these interests.

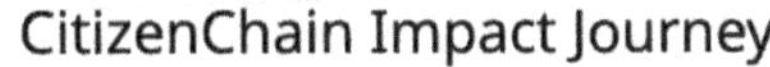

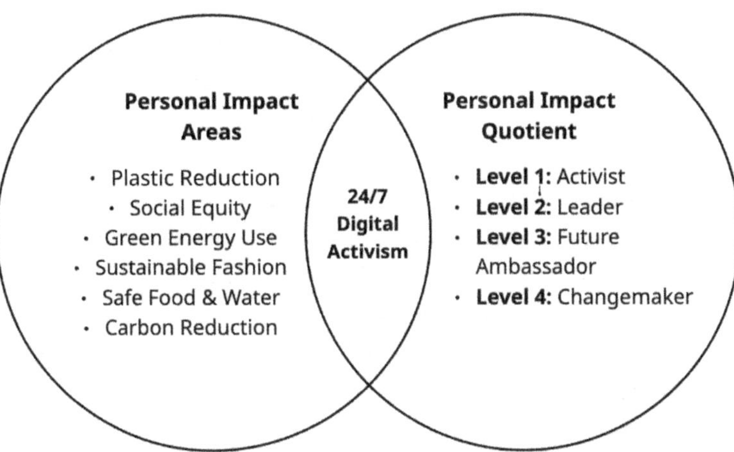

CitizenChain Impact Areas also align with Focus Areas within SustainChain.

Figure 9.4   CitizenChain impact areas align with the focus areas in CitizenChain.

The gameified environment also feeds the network effect by giving impetus to the connections, interactions, and exchanges generated between users. This encourages users to engage through features and experiences that motivate others' participation and contribution. A dynamic network effect facilitates interaction that creates a feedback loop, allowing users to build on each other's contributions. In addition, it continually improves the platform or system to create larger behavioral trends, impacts, and outcomes.

Key Takeaways

Fostering greater awareness and overcoming the human tendency to repeat familiar patterns while expecting different outcomes remain important hurdles on the path to making sustainable change. At the same time, achieving the greatest impact possible will demand more than just maintaining your individual commitment, relying on the proven framework of the changemaker playbook, or leveraging the most advanced technologies to inform, guide, and empower people.

(continued)

(continued)

Ultimately, collective success depends on all who play a necessary role in the solution to step up and fulfill their part: businesses, organizations and coalitions (from big to small), government, and all of us who make up civil society.

Once again, you see how the changemaker process allows you to bring order to your thoughts, temporarily set your disbelief aside, and see that there are smart and simple ways to contribute. If you are particularly passionate and inspired, you can also reach for your sustainability activist weapon. But we don't just need action—we need to actualize the future we want to see by holding ourselves, governments, and businesses to their word. Like its sister platform SustainChain, CitizenChain is designed to help accomplish this by—among many other things discussed in this book—bringing transparency to the actions being taken and, by extension, to those that are not. In this way, these modern and sophisticated uses of technology carry with them a critical way to spot the gaps between stated intentions and impact and become a crucial vehicle for creating accountability.

In so doing, we also enhance our personal capacity to influence the powerful forces that shape the future—especially in areas like public policy and the practices of large corporations—where we feel outsized in our ability to drive change.

Where business is concerned, for-profit companies will naturally focus on their bottom line. However, most know that doing so will over time involve finding solutions to the ways climate will affect their business. By some estimates, 60 percent of firms indicate that climate change has had or is expected to have an observable impact on their revenue, costs, and investments through changing regulations, higher prices for raw materials, and general operating costs (Jargalsaikhan, Leduc, and Oliveria, 2022). As covered in Chapter 5, many companies are showing their strong commitment to being a part of the global solution. At the same time, many are not, and unfortunately that even includes some that *say* they are. It all reinforces the need for sustained action and commitment from members of civil society to continuously utilize the available means to help enforce them.

Regardless of what individual businesses are doing today, there is a critical need to cwollectively urge that they stay focused on making more progress on sustainability, and taking advantage of the most modern and efficient ways to do that. It is simply good business to do so. And CitizenChain is here to do the same for each of us, as individual people who care and want to vote with our pocketbook, our voice, and/or our feet. By taking this action over and over and over again, we let those with the most power and influence know this is a pressure that will only grow stronger, and will not go away.

What makes progress toward mass awareness and continuous engagement so challenging, at its most basic level, is similar to what I discussed at length in many of the previous chapters: the enormous number and fragmented nature of actions already taking place. How to create order and alignment among them, as well as transparency and access to them, is an enormous stumbling block to overcome. The CitizenChain platform—by utilizing much of the same technology as SustainChain—illustrates how the changemaker playbook process, combined with the other tools now in your box, can effectively confront this challenge, and it highlights its value once again as both a path to meaningful impact and a stepping stone toward transformation.

10 | Using Social Media for Good

With playbook in hand, I now turn to the final chapter of the book and a topic that may, ironically, represent one of the greatest sources of hope for having consequential impact than at any time in history: social media. I focus on why and how, as well as the irony of this assertion, and begin by setting the stage with a basic definition:

social media, n.: Herein, refers to websites and applications that focus on communication, community-based input, interaction, content-sharing, and collaboration among users. It enables people to connect, share information, and engage with various communities through text, images, videos, and other content forms.

By now, we are all at least somewhat familiar with the ways that social media has reshaped how people exchange thoughts and experiences with one another. For purposes of completing your playbook, the possibilities that social media may represent to changemakers lie in the impact it's had on our personal behavior and can be seen most readily through the lens of climate change.

As it gets hotter outside and the frequency of climate-related disasters continues to climb, some struggle with the questions of how this has happened or why (whether philosophically, scientifically, or otherwise), but we know it is true intuitively because we are seeing it with our eyes and personally experiencing its effects. Most people feel viscerally that climate change is causing disastrous effects and that we must act at lightning speed to slow the ongoing atmospheric heating. This urgent reality raises the million-dollar question for the current framework, process, and tools: Will they be enough to achieve personal impact and positive change on a massive scale? The answer, which should be clear in this stage of your discovery, is this: When all major elements of the playbook come together, they form a powerful formula for impact, a decisive edge for success, and a genuine source of hope.

However, our collective ability to shift our behaviors will be essential to how much change we can accomplish and certainly the speed at which we can do so. Taking the actions identified through the changemaker process or generated by the intelligence of a platform like CitizenChain has to become a natural and permanent part of our personal routines in order to have their full effect, and this will require that people develop new habits. Just as brushing our teeth in the morning helps prevent cavities, if we are to win the long game on issues like climate change, we need to adopt permanent new behaviors that become a natural part of our daily lives. These actions have to be more or less automatic—in other words, things that the brain-body connection habituates.

brain-body connection, n.: The interplay between thoughts, habits, and physical actions—how our brain and body work together to form automatic behaviors and routines.

I'll pause here to unpack this idea. To create a viable solution, it's useful to consider why developing new habits is so challenging. Anyone who has tried to make healthier choices that don't come naturally, or to break any form of addiction, knows how difficult this can be. Behavior change is hard for many reasons. Every day we all face countless decisions that challenge our ability to consistently choose the best course of action, and we are especially challenged to do so when it requires sustained effort. In addition, positive outcomes are often delayed or intangible (as is the case with reversing climate change), which also makes it harder to stay motivated. When there isn't some form of immediate feedback or gratification, our brains struggle to reinforce consistent behavior.

This is the vein in which I use this chapter to engage in a relatively brief yet critical discussion about social media and how its effects can be used to overcome these challenges.

Setting the Backdrop: The Social Media Phenomenon

In an era that has been defined throughout this book by hyperconnectivity and digital transformation, social media's influence has been extraordinary and unique. Its emergence followed the earliest forms of digital media, starting with a social platform called 6 Degrees in 1997, to be joined by other networks like LinkedIn in 2002, Friendster and Myspace in 2003, and Facebook in 2004. These were just the beginning and would lead to the proliferation of many other platforms that joined, competed, and in some cases replaced them. As this was all happening, consumer and user expectations created a remarkable and steady shift in behavior—creating a hyperfluid, never-ending loop of interaction.

As a consequence, there is little question that social media has been a transformative force that is constantly shaping the way people perceive, interact with, and navigate the world. In addition, because of the billions of users who constantly and actively engage in this activity on numerous platforms simultaneously, social media has become a multifaceted phenomenon, permeating nearly every aspect of modern life. It influences the ways people relate and has redefined personal notions of identity and self-worth. In other words, social media has established a clear capability to connect, inform, and persuade people to act on an unprecedented scale and with incredible velocity.

When you look at social media through this lens, you can begin to see its relevance to the changemaker process and its place in your playbook. Let's delve a little deeper into its capabilities.

Social Media's Value in the Playbook
As established throughout this book, our greatest potential for driving impact lies in the ability to unify our efforts, think differently, and take

persistent action dedicated to constant refinement. To also do this with the greatest effect requires speed, efficiency, and scale. Social media is a modern form of technology, like the others discussed in previous chapters, that can specifically support these key elements, quite possibly through the very behavior changes it has already set into motion—in particular, its highly potent capability to affect the way people think and to inspire constant, continuous, and even unconscious involvement.

In Chapter 1, I introduced the importance of honing an ability to shift your mindset when pursuing consequential action and personal impact—to "retrain" the way you see yourself and the particular role you have in driving massive change. Social media has been continuously reshaping the way we think and act for years. Perhaps it can be used to instill new behaviors and habits that make us all more effective change-makers as well!

Exploring *how* the medium has been successful in molding people's actions and decisions will help you understand this potential more clearly.

Social Media as Weapon for Positive Change: The Irony

When I began to reflect on the remarkable nature of social media in the context of my own playbook, it led me to examine the apparent relationship between the time users spend in a social media setting and the types of action it motivates. Soon after, my focus began gravitating toward a single, unifying thought: Can this relationship become a way to attain the constant and continuous effort needed to overcome our most pressing challenges? Can we apply all there is to learn about the effects of social media to enhance our own natural ability to work smarter, better, and faster together? This ultimately led me to a "full-circle" hypothesis: *Social media may be a 21st-century solution hiding in plain sight.*

While the general significance of social media's effects may be evident, it has a subtler and more pervasive influence that often goes unnoticed. From scrolling through feeds during breakfast to sharing updates before sleep, we now engage with social media reflexively, seamlessly integrating it into our daily routines. In doing so, we unconsciously expose ourselves to a constant stream of information, opinions, and narratives that subtly mold our perspectives and drive our choices. Whether selecting a restaurant, forming opinions on current events, or deciding what causes to support, social media's impact on our day-to-day actions is undeniable. This set of dynamics supports a theory that harnessing its power to effortlessly and unconsciously draw us in can be a way to create a different relationship with delivering consequential impact. By applying these learnings, we can supercharge collective momentum toward positive change, reshape our natural behavior, and create the constant and continuous action needed to address critical global challenges more efficiently than ever before. This is realistic and possible because practical approaches now exist to put it into motion.

Social media has not been without its drawbacks. Indeed, not unlike AI, its reputation as a healthy or ultimately useful phenomenon has been in question for many years. Critics have raised concerns about social media's addictive nature, highlighting how the carefully designed algorithms, notifications, and endless scrolling features can foster compulsive behavior and negatively impact mental well-being. As a result, once-celebrated platforms like Facebook, Instagram, X (Twitter), and many others have faced scrutiny for their role in fostering addiction and promoting superficial interactions that isolate us from meaningful real-world connections. Proceeding with conscious attention to unintended outcomes, then, is also important. If we can do so, within this very potential for addiction also lies an irony: it may also provide the opportunity to create addictive *positive* action and unprecedented impact.

Social media has successfully captivated our attention for personal gain, and the time is now upon us to harness its clear strengths to fuel next-level collective action. By recalibrating the addictive mechanisms to promote informed engagement and constructive involvement, we can convert it into a robust tool for disseminating knowledge, galvanizing support, and orchestrating meaningful initiatives that address complex challenges on a global scale.

By weaving together the dual facets of social media—its capacity for addictive engagement and fundamental behavioral change—we can begin to envision a future where thoughtfully designed social platforms are not just sources of distraction, but instruments of empowerment and groundbreaking progress. In other words, we can navigate the evolving landscape of digital communication, by recognizing the need to leverage what social media can offer and by carefully harnessing its full potential as a force for *good*. With serious and careful thought about how we implement all along the way, we can channel its addictive forces into avenues for education, awareness, and thoughtful action. The goal is to convert social media into a catalyst for positive change and foster a better informed, connected, and engaged society.

Can Social Media Really Help Solve These Issues?

Testing this hypothesis is key, and here again the playbook proves its worth. These facets of social media are already centrally embedded in the way SustainChain and CitizenChain work. The success of these platforms relies on organizations and individuals discovering and joining the platforms, but much more important is how members use them, reflexively and constantly.

Like the communities within them, members need to continuously participate in fluid and dynamic dialogue and action as a direct and natural part of how they personally get things done. Consequently, part of the clean-sheet thinking behind SustainChain and CitizenChain was to imagine each of them as social media platforms like Facebook or LinkedIn. They were created as purpose-driven, highly dynamic environments filled with motivating content, immediately actionable steps, and seamless avenues for collaboration and action.

Here are some specific examples of how manifesting new behaviors in social media-like settings were included in the vision:

- User-generated content can showcase personal achievements, from reduced carbon footprints to sustainable fashion hauls. Businesses, organizations, and individuals can transparently communicate their commitments, achievements, and setbacks, encouraging interaction and continuous improvement.
- Personalized carbon footprint calculators within the platform and tips help reduce emissions in daily life. Real-time updates and success stories foster a sense of urgency and commitment among users. Hashtags and challenges encourage individuals to share their

sustainable practices, amplifying positive behaviors and normalizing eco-friendly choices.

- Brands committed to circular practices can share behind-the-scenes insights into their production processes, demonstrating transparency and accountability. Influencers and users can showcase upcycled, secondhand, and ethically produced fashion, reshaping perceptions of style and consumption. Dedicated hashtags can spotlight innovative circular fashion designs, spurring creativity and sparking conversations about the environmental impact of clothing choices.
- Users can share easily digestible information on water conservation techniques, water-efficient technologies, and the importance of preserving freshwater ecosystems. This can include local water challenges and success stories, thus fostering a global dialogue and encouraging cross-border collaboration.

Unlocking progress in the critical areas I've covered requires collective, urgent action. SustainChain and CitizenChain provide a practical way to leverage the capabilities of this highly sophisticated technology and medium.

Key Takeaways

For the last step in your journey, I have used the final chapter of this book to explain how changemakers can leverage the impact that the social media phenomenon has had on human behavior, as well as how to apply its uniquely powerful capacities to raise the potential of your personal playbook. Like AI and the other tech for good examples laid out in Chapters 5 and 6, there are important reasons to consider social media a key piece of the puzzle for reversing harmful trends like climate change that has been hiding in plain sight for decades.

Indeed, in the digital landscape that it helped fundamentally establish, social media's addictive allure and capability to instill new, natural behaviors represents a galvanizing force for positive change.

Channeling this power through platforms like SustainChain and CitizenChain will create hubs of collective awareness and activism, fostering widespread activity that transcends boundaries and unites people in pursuit of a more sustainable and equitable world. To sum up this piece of the changemaker's formula for success:

Responsible AI + Social media for good = High-velocity intelligence + High-velocity involvement

This approach holds powerful potential to accelerate impact and shape a better future.

Conclusion: Final Words to Changemakers

You have now come to the end of your journey. And as you do, I feel a need to take one more big step back to look at what we've accomplished together. Let's start that reflection by answering a question you may have wondered about as you moved from part to part and chapter to chapter: Why did I write this book? What can I hope to accomplish by passing along this personal playbook for change? These are important questions that deserve answers.

Of all the situations (change opportunities, as you know them now) that I have had the privilege to contribute to, those that had the largest impact also led to my biggest discoveries about what is truly possible. I've discussed many of them as a direct part of building the playbook, but there's more to it. You see, some of what I learned didn't just feel like a discovery. In fact, it felt much closer to an epiphany.

On the discovery side of the equation, the most essential and actionable of insights have been covered at length and addressed throughout the book. The common traits that most problems carry is first among them, and also what drives the playbook's efficacy: every problem is, well, a problem. It's an obstacle to overcome. For each problem, there are underlying reasons—gaps between what *is* and what *you want it to be*. There are interconnected pieces to account for, an order to the steps taken to fix them, and so on.

Without going into them again in too much detail, these steps are part of the overall framework for pursuing impact and making a meaningful and sustained contribution to outcomes that positively affect many people, in many ways, in a world in critical need of them. They can be summed up as follows:

- Look through new eyes.
- Think without artificial constraints (e.g., "it's not possible").
- Get organized.
- Keep an open mind.
- Don't look for all the answers (perfection is a myth).
- Use the most sophisticated tools available to move with knowledge, facility, and speed.
- ACT!
- Observe, learn, refine, repeat; keep your efforts flexible.
- We always get farther, faster, *together*.

I would venture that anyone who adopts this formula with a modicum of resilience and resourcefulness will consistently report positive findings. Quite simply, it works.

And now to revisit the question of "why," and its answer: It was less the many discoveries made throughout the changemaking journey and more the epiphanies—and really just one in particular: At the time I was making these discoveries and realizing their potential benefit, the only thing that would have made them more valuable (that is, have greater impact) was if I'd had them going into my journey as a changemaker instead. I often find myself wondering how much more powerful the impact, faster the progress, and bigger the outcomes might have been if I had a playbook like the one I've passed on to you.

When you put this entire book together and reflect on it in its full form, it is really a book about preparedness and readiness. It proffers that big change, small change, most any change at all comes down to how well-prepared we are to confront the challenge, and act. Preparedness is what gives us the capacity, the confidence, and the courage to take on problems—to dare to become a changemaker. I offer this book in that spirit.

One last note: As expressed in the introduction, I will consider my decision to engage in this effort a worthy one if it inspires you to run toward the opportunities to have personal impact that you encounter, and has you feeling both empowered and emboldened to tap into your inner changemaker. If, as you now finish reading it, you have begun to feel these things and a welling up of personal confidence in your capabilities to walk boldly into the fray, I will consider this book both an honor and a success.

The playbook is now in your hands. It's time to forge ahead into an era where the marriage of technology and human intent shapes a world we can proudly pass on to future generations. So what do you say? Are you ready to go change the world with me?

Changemaker Workbook

This workbook is designed to help you apply the changemaker process to any challenge—personal, business, community, or global. For each exercise, read the prompts carefully and use the space provided to write your thoughts, plans, and reflections. Revisit these exercises as your journey progresses, and remember: the process is as important as the outcome. Take your time, be honest with yourself, and use these pages as a tool for real, step-by-step change.

For inspiration, check out the four complete examples that cover a personal, business, community, and global challenge, respectively.

Part 1: Laying the Foundation: Current Versus Future State

A. Define Your Challenge: Briefly describe a complex problem or area where you want to create change (personal, organizational, or societal):

____

____

____

____

B. Current State Analysis: What is happening now? List the key facts, feelings, or outcomes as they currently exist.

____

____

____

____

C. Future State Vision: Imagine the ideal scenario: What would the situation look and feel like if it were "fixed" or transformed?

____

____

____

____

D. Side-by-Side Comparison Table

Aspect	Current State	Future State (Ideal)
Experience/Outcome		
Processes/Workflows		
Tools/Resources		
People/Stakeholders		
Other		

Part 2: Building the Frame: Gap Analysis and Solution Brainstorm

A. Identify the Gaps: What are the main differences between your current and future state? Where are the disconnects or breakdowns?

____

____

____

____

B. "What's the Fix?" Brainstorm: For each gap, list possible fixes (new tools, changed workflows, new roles, etc.).

Gap/Disconnect	Possible Fixes/Ideas

Part 3: Setting the Plan

A. Prioritize Actions: Which fixes have the most potential for impact? List your top two or three actions to try first:

1. ____
2. ____
3. ____

B. Action Steps and Ownership: For each action, define:

- What exactly will be done?
- Who is responsible?
- What resources are needed?
- What's the timeline?

Action	Who?	Resources Needed	Timeline

Part 4: The Refinement Cycle: Observe, Learn, Refine, Repeat

A. 80:20 Rule Reflection: For your plan, what does "80 percent confidence" look like? What's "good enough" to move forward, even if it's not perfect?

____

____

____

____

B. Weekly Refinement Log: Each week, review:

- What did you try?
- What worked? What didn't?
- What will you adjust for next week?

Week	What I Tried	What Worked	What Didn't	Next Adjustment
1				
2				
3				

Part 5: End-to-End Perspective

Map out the journey from start to finish. Where do handoffs, overlaps, or dependencies exist? Use a simple flowchart or list.

____

____

____

____

Part 6: Key Takeaways and Next Steps

- What did you learn about the power of process in changemaking?
- How does breaking down a big problem into steps make it more manageable for you?
- What will you do next to keep building your changemaker playbook?

____

____

____

____

Bonus: The Long Game Commitment

Write a one-sentence commitment to staying patient and persistent, even when progress is slow:

"I commit to playing the long game by _________________________

____."

Example 1: Personal Level: Improving Work-Life Balance

Part 1: Laying the Foundation: Current Versus Future State

A. Define Your Challenge *Example: I want to achieve a healthier work-life balance because I often feel overwhelmed and have little time for family, friends, or self-care.*

B. Current State Analysis *Example:*

- *I work late most evenings and check emails on weekends.*
- *I rarely exercise or pursue hobbies.*
- *My relationships feel neglected and I'm often tired.*

C. Future State Vision *Example:*

- *I finish work by 6 p.m. most days and unplug on weekends.*
- *I have regular time for exercise, hobbies, and relaxation.*
- *My relationships feel stronger and I have more energy.*

D. Side-by-Side Comparison Table

Aspect	Current State	Future State (Ideal)
Experience/ Outcome	Stressed, fatigued, disconnected	Energized, fulfilled, connected
Processes/ Workflows	No boundaries, reactive to work	Set work hours, proactive planning
Tools/Resources	Work laptop/phone always on	Use "Do Not Disturb" features, planner
People/Stakeholders	Family feels ignored, boss expects 24/7	Family time prioritized, clear boundaries with boss
Other	No "me time" scheduled	Weekly self-care and social time

Part 2: Building the Frame: Gap Analysis and Solution Brainstorm

A. Identify the Gaps *Example:*
- *Lack of boundaries between work and personal time.*
- *No scheduled activities for self-care or relationships.*
- *Expectations from boss and colleagues for after-hours work.*

B. "What's the Fix?" Brainstorm

Gap/Disconnect	Possible Fixes/Ideas
No work/personal boundaries	Set work hours; communicate limits
No time for self-care/hobbies	Schedule weekly exercise/hobby blocks
Boss expects after-hours work	Discuss boundaries; propose coverage plan

Part 3: Setting the Plan

A. Prioritize Actions *Example:*

1. *Communicate new work hours to boss and team.*
2. *Block out two evenings per week for exercise or hobbies.*
3. *Set phone and email to "Do Not Disturb" after 6 p.m.*

B. Action Steps and Ownership

Action	Who?	Resources Needed	Timeline
Communicate work boundaries	Me	Email template	This week
Schedule exercise/ hobby time	Me	Calendar app	Start next week
Set DND on devices after 6 p.m.	Me	Phone settings	Today

Part 4: The Refinement Cycle: Observe, Learn, Refine, Repeat

A. 80:20 Rule Reflection *Example: If I can stick to my new boundaries 80 percent of the time, that's a big improvement—even if I occasionally slip up.*

B. Weekly Refinement Log

Week	What I Tried	What Worked	What Didn't	Next Adjustment
1	Set phone to DND at 6 p.m.	Fewer work interruptions	Still checked email once	Move phone to another room
2	Scheduled hobby time	Enjoyed painting again	Skipped one session	Try morning sessions too

Part 5: End-to-End Perspective

Example: Daily flow:

Workday → End work at 6 p.m. → Exercise or hobby → Dinner with family → Relaxation

Dependencies: Need support from family to respect boundaries; need boss to agree to new schedule.

Part 6: Key Takeaways and Next Steps

Example:

- *Setting boundaries and scheduling personal time helped me feel less stressed.*
- *Progress isn't perfect, but small changes are making a difference.*
- *Next, I'll try a weekend "digital detox" to deepen my work-life balance.*

Bonus: The Long Game Commitment

Example: "I commit to playing the long game by prioritizing my well-being and relationships, knowing that balance requires ongoing effort and adjustment."

Example 2: Community Level: Increasing Access to Healthy Food

Part 1: Laying the Foundation: Current Versus Future State

A. Define Your Challenge *Example: I want to help my neighborhood get better access to affordable, healthy food, since many families rely on convenience stores and have limited fresh options.*

B. Current State Analysis *Example:*

- *The nearest grocery store is two miles away and not easily accessible by public transit.*
- *Most local stores offer mostly processed snacks and sugary drinks.*
- *Community health issues like obesity and diabetes are common.*

C. Future State Vision *Example:*

- *Residents can easily buy fresh fruits and vegetables within walking distance.*
- *Local stores stock more healthy options.*
- *Community health improves and families feel empowered to make nutritious choices.*

D. Side-by-Side Comparison Table

Aspect	Current State	Future State (Ideal)
Experience/ Outcome	Limited healthy food, high health issues	Easy access, improved health, empowered
Processes/ Workflows	Few suppliers, limited store variety	Partnerships with local farms, more options
Tools/Resources	Small stores, no farmers market	Weekly farmers market, food co-op
People/ Stakeholders	Store owners, residents, local officials	Engaged community, new partners
Other	Lack of nutrition education	Regular workshops, school programs

Part 2: Building the Frame: Gap Analysis and Solution Brainstorm

A. Identify the Gaps *Example:*

- *No fresh produce sold locally.*
- *Residents unaware of healthy eating benefits.*
- *No organized effort to address the issue.*

B. "What's the Fix?" Brainstorm

Gap/Disconnect	Possible Fixes/Ideas
No fresh produce locally	Start a community garden or farmers market
Lack of nutrition awareness	Host free workshops and cooking demos
No organized effort	Form a neighborhood food access committee

Part 3: Setting the Plan

A. Prioritize Actions *Example:*
1. *Organize a planning meeting with interested neighbors.*
2. *Reach out to local farmers about starting a weekly market.*
3. *Partner with the community center to offer nutrition classes.*

B. Action Steps and Ownership

Action	Who?	Resources Needed	Timeline
Host planning meeting	Me + volunteers	Flyers, meeting space	Next 2 weeks
Contact local farmers	Me	List of farms, phone	1 month
Set up nutrition classes	Community center	Volunteer instructors	2 months

Part 4: The Refinement Cycle: Observe, Learn, Refine, Repeat

A. 80:20 Rule Reflection *If we can get even one store or market to offer fresh produce, that's a huge step—even if it's not every store yet.*

B. Weekly Refinement Log

Week	What I Tried	What Worked	What Didn't	Next Adjustment
1	Held first planning meeting	Good turnout, strong interest	Some people couldn't attend	Try virtual meeting option
2	Called three local farms	One farm interested	Two didn't respond	Visit farms in person

Part 5: End-to-End Perspective

Example journey:

Identify need → Gather community input → Form committee → Connect with farmers → Launch market → Promote to residents → Evaluate and expand

Dependencies: Need buy-in from store owners, ongoing volunteer support, city permits for market.

Part 6: Key Takeaways and Next Steps

Example:

- *Collaboration is key—many neighbors want to help.*
- *Small wins (like one new produce stand) build momentum.*
- *Next, I'll focus on getting more youth involved and seeking a grant for supplies.*

Bonus: The Long Game Commitment

Example: "I commit to playing the long game by showing up for my community, celebrating small successes, and adapting our approach as we learn together."

Example 3: Business Level: Improving Team Collaboration

Part 1: Laying the Foundation: Current Versus Future State

A. Define Your Challenge *Example: Our team struggles with communication and collaboration, leading to missed deadlines and duplicated work.*

B. Current State Analysis *Example:*

- *Team members often work in silos and rarely share updates.*
- *Meetings are unproductive and lack clear action items.*
- *There is confusion over who is responsible for what.*

C. Future State Vision *Example:*

- *Team members communicate openly and regularly.*
- *Meetings are focused, with clear agendas and follow-ups.*
- *Roles and responsibilities are well-defined and understood.*

D. Side-by-Side Comparison Table

Aspect	Current State	Future State (Ideal)
Experience/ Outcome	Frustration, missed deadlines	Engagement, timely project delivery
Processes/ Workflows	Unclear, ad hoc	Structured, transparent
Tools/Resources	Email only, outdated project tools	Modern collaboration platform
People/ Stakeholders	Team members disengaged	Team feels empowered and connected
Other	Lack of shared goals	Clear, shared team objectives

Part 2: Building the Frame: Gap Analysis and Solution Brainstorm

A. Identify the Gaps *Example:*

- *Lack of real-time communication tools.*
- *No standardized process for meetings or project updates.*
- *Unclear division of responsibilities.*

B. "What's the Fix?" Brainstorm

Gap/Disconnect	Possible Fixes/Ideas
No real-time communication	Implement Slack or Teams
Unproductive meetings	Create meeting templates and agendas
Unclear responsibilities	Develop a RACI chart for all projects

Part 3: Setting the Plan

A. Prioritize Actions *Example:*

1. *Introduce a team messaging platform (e.g., Slack).*
2. *Establish a standard meeting agenda and assign a rotating facilitator.*
3. *Create and share a RACI chart for current projects.*

B. Action Steps and Ownership

Action	Who?	Resources Needed	Timeline
Set up Slack for the team	IT/Team Lead	Slack subscription	2 weeks
Design meeting agenda template	Team Lead	Template, input from team	1 week
Develop RACI chart	Project Manager	Project details, RACI template	2 weeks

Part 4: The Refinement Cycle: Observe, Learn, Refine, Repeat

A. 80:20 Rule Reflection *If 80 percent of meetings are more productive and most team members use Slack, that's a huge improvement—even if not everyone is on board right away.*

B. Weekly Refinement Log

Week	What I Tried	What Worked	What Didn't	Next Adjustment
1	Launched Slack	Quick questions resolved	Some prefer email	Offer Slack training
2	Used new meeting agenda	Meetings stayed on track	Some skipped action items	Assign action item owners

Part 5: End-to-End Perspective

Example: Project flow:

Project kickoff → Assign roles (RACI) → Weekly check-ins (Slack/meetings) → Progress updates → Project completion

Dependencies: Buy-in from all team members, support from IT, ongoing feedback.

Part 6: Key Takeaways and Next Steps

Example:

- *Clear communication tools and processes make a big difference.*
- *Small changes (like a new agenda template) can have a big impact.*
- *Next, I'll gather feedback to further refine our collaboration approach.*

Bonus: The Long Game Commitment

Example: "I commit to playing the long game by continuously seeking feedback, supporting my team, and refining our collaboration practices for lasting success."

Example 4: Global Level: Reducing Local Carbon Footprint

Part 1: Laying the Foundation: Current Versus Future State

A. Define Your Challenge *Example: I want to help my neighborhood reduce its carbon footprint by encouraging more residents to use sustainable transportation options.*

B. Current State Analysis *Example:*
- *Most residents drive alone in gasoline-powered cars for daily commutes.*
- *Public transportation is underused and biking feels unsafe due to lack of bike lanes.*
- *Air quality is declining and traffic congestion is common.*

C. Future State Vision *Example:*
- *Many residents walk, bike, carpool, or use public transit for daily trips.*
- *Safe, accessible bike lanes and improved transit options are available.*
- *Air quality improves and the community feels and healthier and more connected.*

D. Side-by-Side Comparison Table

Aspect	Current State	Future State (Ideal)
Experience/ Outcome	Traffic, poor air quality, isolation	Clean air, less congestion, community
Processes/ Workflows	Default to solo driving	Easy, appealing alternatives
Tools/Resources	Few bike lanes, limited transit info	Bike lanes, real-time transit updates
People/Stakeholders	Drivers, local officials, transit agency	Engaged residents, advocacy groups
Other	Little climate awareness	Regular climate action campaigns

Part 2: Building the Frame: Gap Analysis and Solution Brainstorm

A. Identify the Gaps *Example:*
- *Lack of safe infrastructure for biking and walking.*
- *Residents unaware of environmental impact of driving.*
- *No organized effort to promote alternatives.*

B. "What's the Fix?" Brainstorm

Gap/Disconnect	Possible Fixes/Ideas
Unsafe for biking/walking	Advocate for new bike lanes and sidewalks
Lack of awareness	Launch climate education campaign
No organized effort	Form a "green transportation" neighborhood group

Part 3: Setting the Plan

A. Prioritize Actions *Example:*

1. *Start a petition and meet with city officials about bike lanes.*
2. *Organize a "Car-Free Day" event to raise awareness and encourage alternatives.*
3. *Distribute information on public transit routes and benefits.*

B. Action Steps and Ownership

Action	Who?	Resources Needed	Timeline
Draft petition, collect signatures	Me + volunteers	Petition forms, online tools	3 weeks
Meet with city officials	Group rep	Meeting agenda, data	1 month
Plan Car-Free Day event	Group	Flyers, permits, volunteers	2 months
Distribute transit info	Me	Printed guides, social media	1 month

Part 4: The Refinement Cycle: Observe, Learn, Refine, Repeat

A. 80:20 Rule Reflection *Example: If even 20 percent of residents try a new mode of transport once a week, that's meaningful progress—even if not everyone changes right away.*

B. Weekly Refinement Log

Week	What I Tried	What Worked	What Didn't	Next Adjustment
1	Shared petition at local event	50 signatures collected	Some confusion about goal	Clarify petition message
2	Posted transit info on social media	Positive feedback, shares	Low engagement from older residents	Print flyers for community center

Part 5: End-to-End Perspective

Example: Project flow:

Identify need → Organize group → Petition and advocacy → Infrastructure improvements → Community events → Ongoing education
Dependencies: City council approval, community support, volunteer engagement.

Part 6: Key Takeaways and Next Steps

Example:

- *Small steps (like a petition or event) can spark bigger change.*
- *Collaboration with local officials and residents is essential.*
- *Next, I'll focus on building partnerships with local schools and businesses.*

Bonus: The Long Game Commitment

Example: "I commit to playing the long game by championing climate-friendly choices in my community and celebrating every step forward, no matter how small."

A

More on the DaVinci ML Design

DaVinci is the design, data schema, and development of the machine learning layer that powers the capabilities of SustainChain.

The potential for transformational change that SustainChain represents is defined by the ability of its member community to take all necessary action steps needed to achieve success. Powering SustainChain in this regard is a machine learning and AI capability at its core, called *DaVinci*.

Understanding DaVinci ML and SustainChain

SustainChain is an engine of activity that is dynamically informed by the data its users share. Let's unpack this a bit.

The SustainChain user *experience* utilizes the intelligence that the DaVinci engine generates. Suggested actions are formed through AI algorithms supporting the DV engine; they are served to the SustainChain member community whose actions are guided based on the data attributes supplied by them. Every member action is collected and synthesized, forming a knowledge graph on SustainChain's technical backend.

The overarching objective of DaVinci's is as a capability toolset to maximize and accelerate systems-based action.

Within SustainChain, this takes the form of member and group-level action initiatives (called SAIs), which are pursued by SustainChain members according to their self-ascribed role in the community (e.g., sustainability investor/funder, innovation/solution provider, expert, and so on), industry/supply chain, and sustainability area of focus.

The goal is to unify the sustainability action needed to rebuild global supply chains across these attributes, and to maximize the quantity and velocity of simultaneous action corresponding to six overall sustainability pathways, including:

- Sustainable cities and communities
- Education, gender, and inequality
- Sustainable food, land, water, and oceans
- Health, well-being, and demography
- Energy decarbonization and sustainable industry
- Digital revolution for sustainable development

In summary, SustainChain is a platform that is creating a unified, cross-industry and cross-stakeholder community, where each has visibility to others and they join forces to carry out common activities, goals, and priorities. DaVinci's AI capabilities, then, transform this platform into a revolutionary "change engine" that achieves global sustainability. DaVinci continuously learns from the actions each member takes, cross-references them across the range of attributes, and instantly guides members toward holistic collaboration and action along the six pathways.

Sample DaVinci Recommendations by Member Role Type

This section breaks down example DaVinci recommendations by member role types.

Role 1: Industry Business Leader

This is the chief sustainability officer or director who is responsible for the organization's sustainability goals and objectives:

Goals:

- Find solutions to adopt
- Find partners to team up with on incubating new solutions to their issues

- Discover best practices and existing resources
- See what others with my focus areas/issues are doing about their problems
- Show-off the work (i.e., look good)

Recommendation types:

- Get solutions that match the focus areas (challenges) selected during onboarding
- Get invited to groups where they can learn about what's trending in their focus areas
- Get invited to join action initiatives that are working on their focus areas
- See needs from other members that they may be able to help with, based on matching focus areas
- See leads from other members with matching focus areas
- Be introduced to active members of SustainChain (active = last logged-in last month) that have similar focus areas

Role 2: Sustainability Innovators/Solution Providers

These are startup leaders and executives or leaders at an existing solution provider.

Goals:

- Get exposure and adoption of their solutions/innovations
- Find partners to collaborate with
- See what other innovators are doing in their space
- Find investment opportunities
- Get insight or guidance from academic or thought leaders to advance their innovation

Recommendation types:

- Be introduced to members that are investors that match the focus areas (challenges) they've selected during onboarding

- Get invited to groups where they can learn about what's trending in their focus areas
- Get invited to join action initiatives that are working on their focus or innovation areas
- See needs from other members that they may be able to help with, based on matching focus areas
- See leads from other members with matching focus areas
- Be introduced to active members of SustainChain (active = last logged-in last month) that have similar focus areas
- Suggest creating a call-to-action situation that aligns and acts on your focus areas
- Give a recommend forming a group since several of your focus groups have these action initiatives
- Be guided to post the solution/innovation

Role 3: Social Impact Investor

These are investors.

Goals:

- See what's trending in their areas of focus
- See investment opportunities
- See where there is demand from the community for certain pathways/solutions

Recommendation types:

- See innovators and solution providers that match their focus area
- Get invited to groups that are working on their area of focus
- Get invited to join action initiatives that are working on their focus area
- See needs from other members that they may be able to help with, based on matching focus areas
- See leads from other members with matching focus areas
- Be introduced to active members of SustainChain (active = last logged-in last month) that have similar focus areas
- Be guided to post their investment thesis and budget

Role 4: NGO/Think Tank

These are nongovernmental organizations.

Goals:

- Share their work and expertise and get exposure
- Connect with members with common pathways and goals
- Fundraise

Recommendation types:

- See innovators and solution providers that match their focus area, where they can lend their expertise
- Get invited to groups that are working on their area of focus
- Get invited to join action initiatives that are working on their focus area
- See needs from other members that they may be able to help with, based on matching focus areas
- See leads from other members with matching focus areas
- Be introduced to active members of SustainChain (active = last logged-in last month) that have similar focus areas
- Be guided to post their recent expertise and resources that can benefit the community

Role 5: Academia and Government

This includes key roles in academia and government.

Goals:

- Share their work and expertise
- Connect with members with common pathways and goals
- Fundraise

Recommendation types:

- See innovators and solution providers that match their focus area, where they can lend their expertise

- Get invited to groups that are working on their area of focus
- Get invited to join action initiatives that are working on their focus area
- See needs from other members that they may be able to help with, based on matching focus areas
- See leads from other members with matching focus areas
- Be introduced to active members of SustainChain (active = last logged-in last month) that have similar focus areas
- Be guided to post their recent research and resources that can benefit the community

DaVinci Member Journey

Personalized:

- User = industry business leader versus innovator or funder in an industry, attached to regenerative agriculture as part of pathway 2, and there are 1,000 initiatives going on.
- You've identified your industry as consumer products and your challenge soil health, and there are over 300 initiatives attached to soil health under this regenerative agriculture.
- DaVinci identifies instances/opportunities to consolidate efforts and ways to integrate (across supply chain components, a single supply chain component touching other industries, etc.).

The link between member and sustainability action initiative (SAI) attributes and directed action is driven by a hierarchy. This hierarchy dynamically looks across users with common challenges/solutions/SAIs, user "needs," and efforts/SAIs with a common linkage.

The system is guiding each user by continuously highlighting opportunities to turn common interests and attributes into action, turn like/similar actions into connected/consolidated "ventures," and present unique opportunities—from other industries, geographies, supply chain areas, and so on—to feed and evolve activity occurring on each industry supply chain and SDG pathway.

Sample Member Case

From the actual SustainChain member work on ocean thermal energy. Some companies are creating the capability to supply the energy systems, the experts with the potential to construct the full solution, the government support, the business models to make economically viable, and so on.

These activities are happening simultaneously, and this is where DaVinci comes in—the learning engine is instantly revealing where the connections lie and actions need to be made, where the prioritization must be in order to get to the destination by 2030. Regardless of whether they get there in a way that could be considered absolute, the machine helps systematically guide the actions. The example is an illustration for defining what is needed from each of these players.

The work started with curating member group with the common pathway focus to reduce the carbon footprint, and go beyond offsets and credits to eliminate carbon. Early thoughts:

- Alternative energy is the obvious solution.
- There are a lot of different forms—nuclear, solar, wind, ocean— and there are supply chain components or subcomponents to each but some common ones/overlap.
- Some supply chain components expand the use of OTEC that might touch wind or solar.
- The insight can guide users investing in solar to potentially explore OTEC.
- This systems-based guidance allows users to know things they can't source anywhere else, because DaVinci connects who's in SC with what's happening within it and maps those attributes back to the components that make it viable.

(continued)

(continued)

Notifications linked to certain pathways, or themes/category actions delivered to members as initiations occur; early challenges/blockers alert relevant members as they surface. Some are connected automatically because they're in the system, and some are generated by superuser activity.

In sum, the success that DaVinci generates happens by way of the unique mix of the richness of the data it collects and the ability to link, learn, and suggest new paths in a repeatable way.

Glossary

1 + 1 = 3 effect, **n.:**   An idiom referring to the synergistic relationship of two forces.

30-second spot, **n.:**   A 30-second TV commercial.

80:20 rule, **idiom:**   A principle stating that 80 percent of the outcome for a given event is a result of 20 percent of the input.

algorithm, **n.:**   A series of steps or instructions designed to solve a problem or complete a process. In technology, these instructions are given to a computer for tasks like opening an application, sorting a list of documents, or increasing the brightness on your screen.

artificial intelligence (AI), **n.:**   A vast field of digital tool development utilizing computer systems that are designed to perform complex tasks normally done by human-reasoning, decision-making, creating, and so on.

binge-watching, **v.:**   Continuous watching of a TV show or other form of visual content for a long time without stopping.

brain-body connection, **n.:**   The interplay between thoughts, habits, and physical actions—how our brain and body work together to form automatic behaviors and routines.

connection, **n.:**   The meaningful relationship or bond between people, ideas, and/or efforts that fosters collaboration, understanding, and shared purpose.

consequential action, **n.:**   An action that creates tangible, measurable results.

current state, **n.:**   The present circumstances; the situation as it is now.

***digital media*, n.:** Digitized information displayed or broadcast through a screen, including text, audio, video, and image.

***elixir*, n.:** A catalyst or essential force that energizes and accelerates progress.

***end-to-end*, adj.:** From the very beginning of a process to the very end.

***ethical AI*, n.:** Artificial intelligence systems that prioritize fairness, accountability, transparency, and privacy, ensuring they benefit society and minimize harm and bias.

***future state*, n.:** The situation as it would be in an ideal future scenario.

***gamified*, n.:** An activity, process, or system made more engaging by adding elements typical of games, like points, levels, badges, or rewards to motivate participation and enjoyment.

***hiding in plain sight*, idiom:** Objects or solutions that are easily overlooked due to the simple and uncomplicated nature of their location.

***interactive experience*, n.:** A two-way encounter whereby the viewer is actively involved in what they are shown.

***Leonardo DaVinci*, personal n.:** Innovator, architect, scientist, and one of the most influential artists in history. He left a legacy of groundbreaking contributions in the realms of art, math, science, and architecture, each discipline informing his mastery of the others.

***long game*, n.:** An approach that requires patience and foresight, with the knowledge that a series of smaller, short-term goals must be met before the larger, long-term one can be achieved.

***mission control*, n.:** A centralized hub for monitoring, coordinating, and directing complex operations to ensure successful outcomes.

***network effect*, n.:** As a social phenomenon; a pattern of interconnected individuals who actively exchange information, resources, and support for personal, professional, or communal benefit.

***network-of-networks*, or *super network*, n.:** A group of interconnected networks, which are themselves a group of interconnected people or things.

***operating system*, n:** Software inside a TV that is connected to the internet that lets you use apps, stream shows, and control the TV. It manages how you interact with the TV and what features or streaming services you can access.

***poverty trap*, n.:** A self-reinforcing cycle where extremely poor individuals or countries lack sufficient capital—such as human, business, infrastructure, natural, institutional, and knowledge capital—to make productive investments and escape poverty.

***process*, n.:** A deliberate, step-by-step approach to building something meaningful—like constructing a house, one piece at a time, with each phase depending on the strength and clarity of the previous one. A series of steps with a dedicated goal or desired outcome.

***reinforcement learning (RL)*, n.:** A way for computers to learn by trying things out and seeing what works. The more it practices, the better it is at choosing the actions that lead to the best results. By learning this way, the computer can figure out brand new ways to solve problems—even ones it's never seen before. It can "discover" new paths or strategies to reach its goals, and even adapt if things change.

***resilience*, n.:** The ability to adapt, recover, and thrive amid challenges, disturbances, or adversity, maintaining essential functions and well-being.

***set-top box*, n.:** A device connected to a television to watch cable, satellite, or streaming channels. It takes the signal from your service provider and makes it work with your television.

***single point aggregator*, n.:** A single platform that allows for access to a variety of offerings through one central connection. Instead of dealing with many different providers, you just use the aggregator to reach everything you need in one place.

***software development kit (SDK)*, n:** A set of tools and resources that helps developers build apps for internet-enabled TVs or TV streaming apps without starting from scratch.

***spillover*, n.:** The unintended transfer or impact of effects from one context, activity, or system to another.

***streaming*, n:** A way to watch shows, movies, or live channels over the internet without needing cable or satellite.

***sustainability*, n.:** The capacity to fulfill present needs while safeguarding the environment and ensuring the well-being of future generations.

***white space*, n.:** A term used to describe a solution that has heretofore escaped our discovery or has not yet been successfully implemented.

Works Cited

Abadia, A.F., Yacoub, B., Stringer, N., Snoddy, M., Kocher, M., Schoepf, U.J., Aquino, G.J., Kabakus, I., Dargis, D., Hoelzer, P., Sperl, J.I., Sahbaee, P., Vingiani, V., Mercer, M. and Burt, J.R. (2022). Diagnostic Accuracy and Performance of Artificial Intelligence in Detecting Lung Nodules in Patients with Complex Lung Disease: A Noninferiority Study. *Journal of Thoracic Imaging*, [online] 37(3): 154–161. doi: https://doi.org/10.1097/RTI.0000000000000613.

Bellis, M. (2016). *The History of the Zipper*. [online] ThoughtCo. Available at: https://www.thoughtco.com/history-of-the-zipper-4066245 [Accessed 27 April 2025].

Borgen, C. (2018). *15 Organizations Fighting Poverty in Developing Countries*. [online] The Borgen Project. Available at: https://borgenproject.org/organizations-fighting-poverty-developing-countries/ [Accessed 28 May 2025].

Bundervoet, T. (2016). *Is Africa Still Rising? Taking Stock Halfway Through the Decade*. [online] Brookings. Available at: https://www.brookings.edu/articles/is-africa-still-rising-taking-stock-halfway-through-the-decade/ [Accessed 24 May 2025].

Cecere, C. (2023). *Blog: Computer-aided Farming Helps Grow Crops - ASME*. [online] Asme.org. Available at: https://www.asme.org/topics-resources/content/blog-computer-aided-farming-helps-grow-crops-more-efficiently [Accessed 18 May 2025].

Climate Action Network (n.d.). *Members.* [online]. Available at: https://climatenetwork.org/overview/members/

Clubley, A. (2025). *AI-powered Textile Waste Sorting.* [online] Blue Patch. Available at: https://www.bluepatch.org/ai-powered-textile-waste-sorting/ [Accessed 2 June 2025].

Ding, M. and Gao, Q. (2025). The Impact of Artificial Intelligence Technology Application on Total Factor Productivity in Agricultural Enterprises: Evidence from China. *Economic Analysis and Policy* 86 (June): 399–415. doi: https://doi.org/10.1016/j.eap.2025.03.032.

Drug Target Review (2025). *First AI-designed Drug, Rentosertib, Officially Named by USAN.* [online] Drug Target Review. Available at: https://www.drugtargetreview.com/news/157365/first-ai-designed-drug-rentosertib-named-by-usan/

Enel Group (2025). *Gravitational Storage: Old and New Technologies for Storing Electricity.* [online] Enel Group. Available at: https://www.enel.com/company/stories/articles/2024/03/gravity-storage [Accessed 26 April 2025].

Freeth, T. (2022). *An Ancient Greek Astronomical Calculation Machine Reveals New Secrets.* [online] Scientific American. Available at: https://www.scientificamerican.com/article/an-ancient-greek-astronomical-calculation-machine-reveals-new-secrets/ [Accessed 21 April 2025].

Global Polio Eradication Initiative (2023). *History of Polio.* [online] Polioeradication.org. Available at: https://polioeradication.org/about-polio/history-of-polio/ [Accessed 28 April 2025].

Haneklaus, S., Lilienthal, H. and Schnug, E. (2016). *25 Years Precision Agriculture in Germany - A Retrospective.* St. Louis, Missouri: 13th International Conference on Precision Agriculture.

IBM (n.d.). *Sabre | IBM.* [online] www.ibm.com. Available at: https://www.ibm.com/history/sabre [Accessed 18 May 2025].

IBM (2024). Deep Blue | IBM. [online] www.ibm.com. Available at: https://www.ibm.com/history/deep-blue.

Italy Magazine (2024). *Bologna Celebrates 150 Years of Guglielmo Marconi and His Global Legacy.* [online] Available at: https://www.italymagazine.com/featured-story/bologna-celebrates-150-years-guglielmo-marconi-and-his-global-legacy [Accessed 21 April 2025].

Jargalsaikhan, H., Leduc, S. and Oliveria, L.E. (2022). *How Are Businesses Responding to Climate Risk?* [online] Federal Reserve Bank of San Francisco. Available at: https://www.frbsf.org/research-and-insights/publications/economic-letter/2022/03/how-are-businesses-responding-to-climate-risk/ [Accessed 9 June 2025].

Lead Compound (n.d.). *NCI's Dictionary of Cancer Terms.* [online] National Cancer Institute. Available at: https://www.cancer.gov/publications/dictionaries/cancer-terms/def/lead-compound [Accessed 16 May 2025].

McCann, K. (2025). *How AI is Transforming the Airline Industry.* [online] AI Magazine. Available at: https://aimagazine.com/articles/how-ai-is-transforming-the-airline-industry [Accessed 18 May 2025].

Minderoo Foundation (2017). *Global Plastic Watch.* [online] Global plasticwatch.org. Available at: https://globalplasticwatch.org/about [Accessed 26 April 2025].

Mucci, T. (2024). *History of Artificial Intelligence.* [online] ibm.com. Available at: https://www.ibm.com/think/topics/history-of-artificial-intelligence.

National Geographic (2022). *Isaac Newton: Who He Was, Why Apples Are Falling.* [online] National Geographic Society. Available at: https://education.nationalgeographic.org/resource/isaac-newton-who-he-was-why-apples-are-falling/ [Accessed 26 April 2025].

Nelson, B. (2009). *The Lingering Heat over Pasteurized Milk.* [online] Science History Institute. Available at: https://www.sciencehistory.org/stories/magazine/the-lingering-heat-over-pasteurized-milk/ [Accessed 26 April 2025].

Radage, K. (2024). *A Study on Contactless Payments by Country.* [online] Credit Card Processing and Merchant Account. Available at: https://www.clearlypayments.com/blog/a-study-on-contactless-payments-by-country/.

Sachs, J. (2005). *The End of Poverty: Economic Possibilities for Our Time.* New York: Penguin Books.

Salk Institute for Biological Studies (2015). *About Jonas Salk: Salk Institute for Biological Studies.* [online] Salk Institute for Biological Studies. Available at: https://www.salk.edu/about/history-of-salk/jonas-salk/ [Accessed 28 April 2025].

Santos, R., Ursu, O., Gaulton, A., Bento, A.P., Donadi, R.S., Bologa, C.G., Karlsson, A., Al-Lazikani, B., Hersey, A., Oprea, T.I. and Overington, J.P. (2016). A Comprehensive Map of Molecular Drug Targets. *Nature Reviews Drug Discovery* 16(1): 19–34. doi: https://doi.org/10.1038/nrd.2016.230.

Shaw, A. (2011). *Breaking Through: Millennium Villages Project Year 5.* Millennium Villages Project.

Silver, D., Hubert, T., Schrittwieser, J. and Hassabis, D. (2018). *AlphaZero: Shedding New Light on Chess, Shogi, and Go.* [online] Google DeepMind. Available at: https://deepmind.google/discover/blog/alphazero-shedding-new-light-on-chess-shogi-and-go/.

TeamStage (2022). *Volunteering Statistics for 2022: How Charitable Are We?* [online] TeamStage. Available at: https://teamstage.io/volunteering-statistics/ [Accessed 28 May 2025].

UNDP (2024). *The World's Largest Survey on Climate Change Is Out—Here's What the Results Show.* [online] UNDP Climate Promise. Available at: https://climatepromise.undp.org/news-and-stories/worlds-largest-survey-climate-change-out-heres-what-results-show [Accessed 9 June 2025].

Uri, J. (2020). 50 Years Ago: *"Houston, We've Had a Problem."* [online] NASA. Available at: https://www.nasa.gov/history/50-years-ago-houston-weve-had-a-problem/ [Accessed 6 May 2025].

World Bank Group (2024). *Ending Poverty for Half the World Could Take More Than a Century.* [online] World Bank. Available at: https://www.worldbank.org/en/news/press-release/2024/10/15/ending-poverty-for-half-the-world-could-take-more-than-a-century [Accessed 28 May 2025].

World Bank (2024). *Poverty, Prosperity, and Planet Report 2024.* [online] World Bank. Available at: https://www.worldbank.org/en/publication/poverty-prosperity-and-planet [Accessed 28 May 2025].

World Health Organization (2021). *History of Polio Vaccination.* [online] World Health Organization. Available at: https://www.who.int/news-room/spotlight/history-of-vaccination/history-of-polio-vaccination [Accessed 28 April 2025].

Zewe, A. (2025). *Explained: Generative AI's Environmental Impact.* [online] MIT News. Available at: https://news.mit.edu/2025/explained-generative-ai-environmental-impact-0117.

Acknowledgments

This book is the culmination of a 35-year journey shaped by the extraordinary people and experiences that have made me who I am as a changemaker.

From the very first days of my professional life, I have been guided by the wisdom of my Columbia University professor Henry Graff, whose words urging me to "Stay on the mark" and "Know exactly what you will do with an opportunity to have impact if you are fortunate enough to get one" have been a touchstone throughout my adult life. Professor Graff's guidance instilled the importance of clarity, purpose, and resolve, and shaped my approach to every major opportunity and challenge I've been blessed to have.

Among the many individuals who have profoundly influenced my journey, I owe a particular debt of gratitude to Paul Allen. The opportunities Paul gave me at the very start of my career, and the original frameworks he developed, are alive and woven throughout the approaches I share in these pages. I learned the value of intellectual curiosity, remaining driven yet patient, and, above all, of never losing sight of the big picture.

I am also deeply grateful to Professor Jeffrey Sachs, whose faith in my ability to apply these lessons on a global scale—particularly in the arenas of economic development and sustainability—led to some of my deepest revelations about what's possible and what it takes to effect lasting change in highly complex circumstances. These learnings have been the source of some of the most important refinements to my practice and have made it possible to pass them on to others.

The confidence that grew from my successes and failures over these many years has been a wellspring of personal growth, that continues to push me to discover the full extent of my capabilities.

Building BrightLine has been one of the most rewarding chapters of my career, and I could not have done it without Robert Aksman. His partnership and many years of commitment were essential as we navigated the many twists and turns of the media industry. My heartfelt thanks go as well to fellow founders JR McKechnie and Chris Redpath, to Michael Bologna for his fresh energy and wonderful leadership, the entire BrightLine team, who embody the very best a CEO could hope for, and to our clients, partners, and investors, whose steadfast belief in our vision has fueled our progress and success.

I am blessed to be surrounded by wise and steadfast friends who have walked arm in arm with me on this journey—Joanna Rubenstein, Amina Mohammed, Carmen Effron, Joan Hornig, Julia Perry, Joanna Hall, and many others. Their wisdom, friendship, and presence have taught me to see strengths in myself that I might never have recognized otherwise, and to act on them. Thank you to Joan Hornig, in particular, who has been a guiding force in the creation of this book; without her it might never have been written.

To my cherished family—Patricia Panepinto, Catherine Gringer, Karen Valle, Celia Puccio, Jeanette Attardi, Vito Pricola, Ricky Palermo—and my dear friends—the Martin Roslev/Lykke Bellum family, Laura Zahn, Katie Brown, Art Allen, JoAnn and Mark Alexander, Liz Marks, Chris Carey, Sonia Sachs, Linda Yaccarino, Patricia Allen, Mitra Best, Phoebe Koundouri, and so many others: your kindness, laughter, and constant support have enriched my life and helped shape these pages.

Most of all, to my husband, Mark, and our three beautiful daughters—Kaitlyn Rose, Kristiana Grace, and Alexandra Maria—you are my greatest inspiration. Your love and support have been the foundation that has allowed me to stay true to the path of change. Thank you for believing in me, and for inspiring me every single day. And a very special thank you to my daughter Kaitlyn for the hours, energy, and literary skill she dedicated to supporting me in my writing process.

Finally, Liz Elting and Victoria Savanh, thank you for believing in the value of writing a how-to book for creating change, to the whole team at Wiley, and to Gabriella Claire, Jenny Thompson, and all who have been part of this journey—thank you. This book is as much yours as it is mine.

About the Author

Jacqueline "Jacquie" Corbelli is an inspirational leader, entrepreneur, and author whose transformational approach to problem solving has made a positive impact on business and the world across her decades-long career. Her work across finance, advertising, technology, sustainability, and global development have proven time and again that her consistent framework combined with passion, innovation and persistence yields tremendous results and world-scale change.

As the first female founder of an advertising technology company and creator of an AI-powered sustainability platform, Jacquie has fueled the success of her companies and been recognized for her groundbreaking leadership by *New York Business Journal* and *Fast Company*. Jacquie has partnered with institutions such as the **United Nations** and the **Vatican**, bringing her expertise to some of the world's most pressing challenges. Jacquie has been featured in the *Wall Street Journal*, *Bloomberg Business*, and *Fox Business*. She lives in New York with her husband, daughters, and dog, and can be seen around the world doing important work in service to others.

Index